Home Fermentation

Home Fermentation

A STARTER GUIDE

Katherine Green

SONOMA
PRESS

Contents

PART 1: A QUICK FERMENTATION EDUCATION

PART 2: THE RECIPES

Introduction

I have always loved pickles—like, seriously loved pickles. When I was in college, I studied in Tokyo for a year, and my passion for these salty, sour treats only grew. I became obsessed with *tsukemono*, the wildly varied but always delicious Japanese pickles offered in small servings at nearly every traditional meal, whether for breakfast, lunch, or dinner. Sometimes, you even find them at the bar. I specifically remember the *takuan*, a type of fermented daikon. When I traveled to a mountain town near Nagano, it was served with every meal. I can still see it in my mind almost 20 years later.

After I returned home, I began making pickles, following a couple of basic recipes I had learned in Japan. I then did what any self-respecting 21-year-old would do: I turned to making wine. I began fermenting gallons of grape juice regularly in the closet of my small apartment. At first, I was kind of nervous to drink the wine I made. Like most people who begin making something new, I had lots of questions—and this was long before the fermenting movement really got off the ground, and before the Internet provided millions of answers to every query.

I spent loads of time at a local home brew shop picking the brain of the owner, and scoured available magazines to ensure that the wines I produced would be both palatable and nontoxic. After all, safety is everyone's concern when making fermented foods and beverages. Today, over 15 years later, I understand a lot more about the science behind fermentation than I did back then, and I can assure you that fermentation is not nearly as difficult or daunting a task as it may seem.

In 2005, I was working for a large Internet company in Los Angeles and was sent to India for six months, a trip that would greatly change the course of my life. There I was introduced to some of the most amazingly complex fermented foods I have ever tasted. Living in South India, I ate fermented bean and rice staples like *idli* and *dosa* on a daily basis, and topped foods with a wide variety of fermented condiments, my favorite of which is still coconut chutney. I learned to cook countless dishes from my colleagues, and when I returned, I began tinkering again with the fermentation of food, and have been at it year-round ever since.

Fermentation is a bug, and once you get it, it's hard to shake it. It's an unfamiliar world that quickly becomes familiar with a little experimentation. In this book, I'll begin by explaining important fermentation basics, so

you understand not only what you are doing, but how to tell when you are finished and how to troubleshoot any problems that may arise along the way.

I'll then walk you through more than 100 ferments you can create in your kitchen right now. Arranged by type, this guide spends plenty of time on vegetables and fruits before moving on to dairy, grains, and, everyone's favorite, beverages. Designed with the user in mind, this book will help you home in on exactly what you want to make and then guide you every step of the way.

The first two chapters provide tons of practical information, from what supplies and utensils you will need to the nuts and bolts of the general fermentation process. Whether you are new to fermenting or have several projects under your belt, this section provides an excellent primer. Before moving on, be sure to try out the simple sauerkraut recipe in chapter 3 (page 41)—it details the steps of fermentation applicable to nearly every project in the book.

I love to teach, and am thrilled to be able to share my knowledge of home fermenting with you. For me, the most rewarding part of teaching is when participants have that "aha" moment. And no doubt, it will be coming for you shortly. So get ready to dive in and have some fun!

Part 1 A Quick Fermentation Education

CHAPTER ONE

Let's Get Cultured

Fermentation is an ancient practice, and one that has taken place for centuries in places with much less sanitation than any modern-day kitchen. While food safety is important, you should rest assured that fermentation is a safe practice that need not be approached with fear. On the contrary, it is a fun, exciting, and delicious way to get the most from your harvest. Armed with the knowledge in this chapter, you will gain the confidence to begin fermenting a wide variety of foods with ease.

FERMENTATION BASICS

During fermentation, the naturally occurring sugars in fruit, juice, milk, or vegetables are transformed into lactic acid, acetic acid, or alcohol. This transformation occurs thanks to the growth of bacteria, yeast, or molds on these food products, which either can be added to the ferment or are naturally present in the environment where the fermentation is taking place.

During the fermentation process, food is broken down from its original state, creating a new product altogether. Firm and crunchy cabbage becomes tender. Sweet and flavorful juice becomes wine. Hard apple cider transforms into pungent vinegar. Depending on the desired outcome, different processes are used for culturing or fermenting these foods.

Lacto-Fermentation

Lacto-fermentation is the process used in the majority of recipes in this book. While the word "lacto" may bring to mind milk, in this case the term refers to lactic acid. In this process, *Lactobacillus* bacteria convert the sugar found in plants into lactic acid, which then preserves the food. Salt or starter cultures are added to protect the foods before spoilage bacteria, yeasts, and molds, also found in the air around us, take hold. This is the type of fermentation used to make pickled foods such as sauerkraut, cucumber pickles, and kimchi, as well as many of the fruit ferments in this book.

Acetic Acid Fermentation

Fermentation used to make vinegar is called acetic acid fermentation. This type of fermentation allows *Acetobacter* bacteria to feed on ethanol and transform it into an acidic, soured condiment. It is thought that vinegar was first produced by accident in the process of making wine, but it has since become a regular ingredient in cuisines around the world. Modern methods for vinegar making have reduced the process from months to just 24 hours in a controlled environment. To make the vinegars in this book, we use wild fermentation, which draws on *Acetobacter* bacteria present in the air around us.

Alcohol Fermentation

Traditionally, alcohol fermentation was managed with wild yeasts. Today, commercially produced yeasts are responsible for much of the production of beer and wine. Varying strains of yeast are used to inoculate the juice, feed on its sugars, and transform them into ethanol. In beer and wine making, the most common types of yeast used are strains of *Saccharomyces cerevisiae*.

WHY FERMENT?

Initially, fermenting was a means for extending the harvest. In a time long before refrigeration, fermenting was widely employed to prolong the period people could keep their produce edible. It was developed out of need, not for its health benefits. If only our ancestors knew what they had stumbled upon

FERMENTED, PICKLED, OR BOTH?

In some cases, the terms "fermenting" and "pickling" can be used synonymously, while in others they cannot. Confused? Well, here's the difference:

- -

Fermenting is a process of transforming a food item using bacteria, yeast, or mold to produce acid or alcohol. This process makes beer, wine, and mead, as well as cheese, vinegar, kefir, kombucha, pickles, sauerkraut, and kimchi. From that list, pickles, sauerkraut, and kimchi are the only items that are considered pickled as well as fermented. As you can see below, many fermented foods are not pickled at all.

FERMENTED ONLY:

Sourdough bread • Kombucha • Kefir • Beer • Wine

- -

Pickling, on the other hand, can include both fermented pickled foods like those noted above, as well as myriad other foods made through a different process called acidification. This type of pickling includes foods that are soured by adding vinegar or another acid to them. These types of foods are sometimes called quick-pickled foods.

PICKLED ONLY:

Refrigerator dill pickles • Dill relish • Other pickles made with vinegar

- -

In addition, many of the same items that are pickled can be made through both quick-pickling and fermentation.

BOTH FERMENTED AND PICKLED:

Fermented dill pickles • Sauerkraut • Kimchi • Lacto-fermented relishes and chutneys

when they decided to salt those vegetables for the first time!

In recent years, an increased awareness has developed about the body's gut flora and its ability to help improve one's overall health. Because of this, along with a growing industry of probiotic products for sale everywhere you look, the interest in fermentation has risen exponentially as people work to bring their diet back to the earth. Aside from being a trendy hobby with tasty results, food fermenting boasts many practical and health benefits. Here are some of the most compelling reasons to get started with home fermentation:

Extended Shelf Life

It really comes down to this: fermenting foods buys you more time. While the shelf life of most produce naturally hovers around a week, fermenting those same foods can allow you to store them for a month or more. This added time allows you to enjoy your vegetables and fruits without losing them to spoilage. And if you ferment your favorites, chances are you will still have some perfectly viable products tucked away in the refrigerator when their season has passed.

Bodies in Balance

Fermented foods contain healthy probiotic bacteria that help colonize your small intestine. Here they do all their great work, including preventing pathogenic bacteria from flourishing, improving nutrient absorption, and easing digestion. Keeping everything in balance, these healthy bacteria give your body a break, while still allowing your system to stay well nourished. This is not the case with many store-bought fermented foods that may have been fermented in their initial production but are actually pasteurized to extend shelf life. This heat-processing step minimizes nearly all the probiotic benefits of these foods.

Waste Reduction

If you are already eating store-bought fermented foods such as kombucha, kefir, and pickles, you may have grown tired of the continual packaging waste. When you ferment at home, you eliminate this waste since you can reuse the same jars and bottles for storing your home-crafted foods. Plus, since preservation extends the shelf life of your foods, you'll notice that you have less spoilage and therefore less food waste.

All the Flavors

When you make cultured foods yourself, you are able to control which ingredients you put in them, ultimately making the finished product exactly what you like. This control over your food allows you to let your taste buds take the reins in creating foods suited just to you and your preferences. While you need to adhere to certain basics, like the ratio of salt or starter culture to water, including add-ons like spices and herbs can give your homemade ferments your own individual touch.

HOMEMADE SAVINGS

While you won't get the instant gratification of grabbing a product off the shelf, you will receive the ultimate payback for your hard work: a plethora of ferments for a fraction of the cost. One of the best reasons to ferment foods yourself is the cost savings. If you buy produce in season, it's much lower in price, and since you do the labor yourself, you are not paying someone else to prepare your food.

Eden Foods Organic Sauerkraut: $6
HOMEMADE SAUERKRAUT: $0.70

GT's Raspberry Chia Kombucha: $3.29
HOMEMADE RASPBERRY CHIA KOMBUCHA: $0.30

Bubbies Dill Pickles: $5.99
HOMEMADE DILL PICKLES: $1.10

Vermont Creamery Crème Fraîche: $4.99
HOMEMADE CRÈME FRAÎCHE: $0.55

Bragg Apple Cider Vinegar: $4.99
HOMEMADE APPLE CIDER VINEGAR: $0.50

Money in Your Pocket

If you have a kombucha or kefir habit, you know how quickly these products can drain your pocketbook. So, unless you are prepared to pay $3 to $4 per bottle daily, fermenting these drinks at home is a great way to go. Not only can you produce products that rival commercial ones, you can also make several bottles for a fraction of the cost of commercial brands.

Take It Easy on Your Body

Fermented foods have begun the process of breaking down, making it easier for your body to digest them. Some people, especially those who have sensitivities to certain grains or even milk, find that the fermenting process allows them to eat foods they otherwise could not tolerate. And for everyone, eating fermented foods regularly can have a big impact on improved digestion overall.

THE BEST FOODS FOR BEGINNERS TO FERMENT

The best foods to begin fermenting are the ones you most enjoy. After all, you don't want to ferment something you won't want to eat. That being said, the 10 ferments listed below are some of the easiest to get started with—they are all beginner level and pretty simple to get right the first time. Most of the items on the list are rather quick ferments, but don't let the longer fermentation times required for some of the others scare you off. There is relatively little work required for the longer ferments once you complete the initial steps—they simply use harder vegetables that take more time to transform into fermented delights.

FERMENTED FOOD	FERMENTATION TIME
Kefir (page 125)	24 hours
Lacto-Fermented Berries (page 97)	1 to 2 days
Strawberry-Mint Chia Jam (page 101)	1 to 2 days
Lacto-Fermented Raspberry-Mint Syrup (page 99)	2 days
Water Kefir (page 200)	2 to 3 days
Nectarine-Blackberry Kvass (page 213)	2 to 3 days
Classic Kimchi (page 64)	3 to 5 days
Fermented Carrots (page 82)	5 to 7 days
Sourdough Starter (page 149)	6 days
Basic Sauerkraut (page 41)	2 to 6 weeks
Apple Cider Vinegar (page 169)	1 to 2 months

FERMENTING WITH KIDS

Fermentation is like one big science experiment, and one that can really enliven the imagination of children. I have been fermenting with my kids since they were tiny, and they have grown to love both the fermented foods we create and the process itself. If you have children, I urge you to get into the kitchen with them and try some of the recipes in this book together.

Chopping hard foods like cabbage is definitely not suitable for young kids, but measuring, weighing, mixing, and packing ferments into jars are totally doable as they become capable. This is a fun, hands-on way that they can get involved in the kitchen. Just make sure they wash their hands really well before beginning.

Also interesting to note is that kids are very adaptable, and if you introduce fermented foods early on, they are more likely to enjoy eating them as they get older. My youngest son has loved eating sauerkraut by the spoonful since he was about two, and really enjoys being involved in the process of making it. Here are some of the things I do to get my kids involved:

• Bring out a variety of whole spices for them to smell, and then let them help me determine how we should season a ferment.

• Give them a job of their own, such as stirring or measuring, allowing them to work together and have ownership over their role.

• Have tasting times, when they can sample many items at once, including those still fermenting, to test for doneness.

THE PLUSES OF PROBIOTIC FOODS

As probiotic foods have become more popular, so has the influx of research detailing their health benefits. While the data is not entirely conclusive at this point, major health organizations, such as the Mayo Clinic and the Academy of Nutrition and Dietetics, state that positive health benefits are associated with eating fermented foods. While we don't yet have definitive proof, enough compelling evidence at this point demonstrates that eating fermented foods can help create balance in your body.

Despite what many advertisers would lead you to believe, however, fermented foods are not the silver bullet to better health. Rather, eating them on a regular basis is a positive step in your quest for overall well-being. Following are some of the most compelling reasons to eat these probiotic foods made through fermentation.

Improve Digestion

Probiotic foods are loaded with healthy bacteria that travel through your digestive system and colonize your small intestine. These bacteria can be particularly helpful for reducing inflammation in the gut, a condition that occurs with diarrhea, gastroenteritis, irritable bowel syndrome (IBS), and cancer. While it remains unclear which strains of bacteria are the most beneficial, it is evident that these foods are effective in maintaining good gut health. As little as one spoonful of sauerkraut a day is all you need to begin on the path toward improved digestion.

Prevent Infection

Lactobacillus and other good strains of bacteria are thought to protect against common food-borne pathogens such as *Listeria monocytogenes*, *Bacillus cereus*, and *Staphylococcus aureus*. While it is not thoroughly understood how this occurs, the belief is that bacteriocins produced by *Lactobacillus* bacteria inhibit other strains, such as these pathogenic bacteria.

Increase Immunity

Beyond foodborne illness, fermented foods are thought to provide increased immunity from everyday occurrences such as the common cold and flu. Again, there is no conclusive evidence for this as yet, but in my experience, which includes eating fermented foods nearly every day for many years, I rarely get so much as a cold, even while nursing sick children back to health.

Improve Mental Health

Recent evidence published in the journal *Psychiatry Research* makes a connection between eating fermented foods and mental health. The research indicates that people who consume fermented foods suffer from less social anxiety than those that do not. So, if social anxiety is a problem for you, load up on sauerkraut and pickles and see what they can do!

While more research is needed in all these areas to more thoroughly understand the connections, there is enough compelling

- -

FAQ Can I Get Sick from a Bad Ferment?

Technically, you probably could make yourself sick with a bad ferment. However, just as when preparing other foods, you must use your best judgment and solid reasoning to make an informed decision. As I show you throughout this book in a number of troubleshooting charts, if a ferment is bad, there are plenty of clues to prevent you from eating it.

Smell is perhaps the most telling factor. If something smells putrid or foul, simply do not eat it. When making ferments like sauerkraut, there are also troubleshooting tips for things like mold that allow you to just remove the moldy kraut and continue fermenting. Whenever these safe practices are available for the type of food you are fermenting, I will let you know, as this knowledge greatly diminishes the chances that you will make a wrong decision when it comes to the safety of your home-fermented foods.

evidence that these traditional foods are beneficial for you. And they taste great, so there is no reason not to give them a try.

FERMENTATION METHODS

Wild Fermentation

Wild fermentations do not use any culture to start; instead they rely on bacteria and yeast already present in the environment around us. To facilitate this without spoilage, wild ferments typically use salt or another agent to prevent the growth of harmful bacteria during fermentation. Salt inhibits the growth of spoilage organisms, draws the moisture out of foods, and helps ensure that the process is effective.

- **Dry-salting.** Dry-salting is used on foods that can produce their own liquid when salted. The best-known food made by this method is sauerkraut, which typically makes use of wild fermentation to make the transformation from cabbage. Once salted, the moisture is drawn out of the cabbage and creates a brine for fermentation.

- **Brining.** For foods that cannot create a brine on their own, such as cucumbers, garlic, or carrots, the brining method is used instead. In this method, water is mixed with salt, whey, or another starter culture and poured over the vegetables or fruits. Brining can be used for both wild fermentation and starter fermentation.

Starter Fermentation

Starter fermentation is an alternative method of fermentation most often used when one is looking to minimize the use of salt, especially in fruit ferments where salt would be undesirable. Starter fermentation works by acidifying the food to protect it. Then the food is inoculated with a culture that works to ferment the food. A wide variety of starters can be used for this type of fermentation:

- **Whey.** Whey is a clear liquid that remains after separating the curds from milk. It is typically drained from kefir or milk for use as a starter culture. Whey produced as a by-product of cheese making is not suitable for use as a starter culture, as it has been heated above the point that the beneficial bacteria die.

- **Dried starter cultures.** Several types of commercially prepared starter cultures are available, the most common being Caldwell's. These are especially great for fermenting fruits and vegetables. Added by the spoonful to water, these cultures are easy to use and produce fermented foods loaded with probiotics, but without all the salt.

- **Other liquids.** One can use other pickling liquids to get a ferment going, such as kombucha, water kefir, and pickling brine. These work to acidify the food's environment and prevent the growth of harmful mold, yeast, and bacteria, while inoculating the vegetables or fruit with the healthy bacteria they need to begin fermenting.

SEASONAL GARDENING FOR YEAR-ROUND ENJOYMENT

 While you are ramping up to begin fermenting, you may want to try your hand at gardening, too. Many of the foods fermented in this book can be easily grown at home, for an even lower total cost. Additionally, when you grow foods yourself you can ensure that they are organic, fresh, and the highest in quality. Here are some of the best items to grow at home:

- -

Cucumbers. It may seem like cucumbers need a lot of space, but the truth is you can easily trellis them upward, and even grow them in large pots on a sunny porch or balcony. When you grow cucumbers at home, you know you are getting them completely fresh and have control over the variety, which, depending on where you live, may not be otherwise available to you. You can make small batches of pickles with just one plant, while several plants will give you a steady supply all summer. Be sure to water cucumbers well, especially once cucumbers are present on the plants, to prevent them from becoming bitter.

- -

Tomatoes. Tomatoes are also easy to get going, whether in pots or in the ground. For fermentation in recipes such as salsa, grow paste tomatoes to create a less watery product. Fertilize the plant(s) once or twice during the growing season, and you'll have a steady supply of tomatoes throughout the heat of the summer.

- -

Herbs. If nothing else, try your hand at growing herbs. They are super easy to grow—and homegrown sure beats paying the premium prices at the grocery store. Mint, cilantro, basil, rosemary, thyme, and oregano can all be grown either in pots or in the ground. A benefit of growing herbs in pots is that you can bring them indoors in the winter and continue growing them near a sunny window. Even if you are just adding them here and there to ferments, having these on hand saves a lot of money over time, and requires less to remember when you are going to the store.

- **Other cultures.** For some of the recipes in this book, including kefir, kombucha, water kefir, and yogurt, you will need additional cultures to begin. For kefir and water kefir, you will need kefir and water kefir grains; for kombucha, you will need a SCOBY (more on this later!); and for yogurt, you can use plain yogurt with live cultures from your local grocery store to get started. All these ingredients are available online, and depending on where you live, you may also be able to find them locally. Check out the Resources section at the back of the book (page 219) for more information on where to purchase these items.

SPROUTING AND SOAKING: GETTING THE MOST FROM LEGUMES, NUTS, GRAINS, AND SEEDS

Many additional practices can be carried out in your kitchen to improve the digestibility of the foods you eat every day. Two of the most common and beneficial ferments you can start right now with no fancy equipment are sprouting and soaking.

Some foods, such as legumes, grains, and seeds, benefit from sprouting before use. This simple process increases their nutritional value by making them more digestible. Sprouting is an ancient practice used by many civilizations before us, and has been shown to drastically change the composition of these foods. By sprouting legumes, grains, and seeds, you produce vitamin C and increase the vitamin B content of these foods. In grains, sprouting is particularly beneficial, as it decreases phytic acid, a compound that prevents the absorption of minerals such as magnesium, iron, zinc, and calcium. Sprouting also creates enzymes beneficial to digestion and helps the body efficiently digest the carbohydrates that make up all these foods.

To get started with sprouting, all you need is a quart jar, a jar ring, and a sprouting screen. A sprouting screen is a small food-safe plastic or stainless-steel screen that fits over the mouth of a mason jar to allow for airflow during sprouting. You can find one online or at a local store that sells fermentation, canning, or sprouting supplies.

Even if you don't want to sprout legumes, grains, and seeds, it's always a good idea to

- -

FAQ Can Pregnant Women Eat Fermented Foods?

Not only can pregnant women eat fermented foods, many natural health practitioners encourage the practice, as it can be beneficial to the health of both mom and baby. While some ferments, like those that are alcoholic, should be avoided, most others are perfectly fine to continue eating throughout pregnancy. Kefir, sauerkraut, and pickles are among these products. If you have concerns about consuming any fermented product during pregnancy, talk to your doctor.

SPROUTED RADISH AND BROCCOLI SEEDS

Starting with a handful of seeds, you can grow lush sprouts in just 3 to 5 days. I like this combination of broccoli and radish seeds, which produces a versatile and spicy blend of sprouts. Be sure to buy seeds from a reputable vendor that sells them marked "for sprouting." As the seeds sprout, they come to life and provide beneficial enzymes and nutrients. Try this project with kids of any age—watching the transformation is as fun for them as it is for you.

3 tablespoons broccoli and/or radish seeds

1 Place the seeds in a quart jar and add enough water to cover them by a couple of inches. Affix a sprout screen and jar ring to the jar and swirl the water around. Drain the water. Cover the seeds again in water by about 2 inches, and leave the seeds to soak overnight.

2 The following morning, drain the water from the seeds. Add fresh water to cover the seeds again, swirl the seeds in the jar, and drain. Prop the jar upside down and at a slight angle over a bowl so that the water drains from the seeds and they do not stay wet. (Rather, they slowly dry until the next rinsing.)

3 Continue filling the jar with water, swirling the seeds, draining them, and then propping the jar upside down at an angle 2 to 3 times per day for the next 3 to 5 days. The seeds will sprout and continue to grow over the next several days, and will soon fill the jar. When this occurs, they are done and need to be stored. It's best to store them when they are thoroughly dry, so if they are approaching this stage, wait to rinse them and let them air-dry for storage. Transfer the sprouts to the refrigerator to store.

MAKES 1 QUART

Prep: **5 minutes, plus 5 minutes daily** | Sprouting: **3 to 5 days** | Storage: **5 days**

- -

MAKE IT A MEAL: *Sprouts can increase the flavor and nutritional value of just about any meal. Try them in all types of sandwiches, wraps, and salads for some unexpected crunch. They are well matched with meat dishes, where their somewhat spicy flavor plays well with both red meats and poultry alike. They can even be great on soup for a crisp topping with a little bite.*

SPROUTED HUMMUS

Hummus is readily available at every supermarket these days, but it is so easy to make at home that it just doesn't make sense to buy it packaged at the store. Sprouting takes a few days, but it is well worth the minimal effort required. The resulting hummus is super creamy, flavorful, and easy on the stomach.

½ cup dried chickpeas
2 garlic cloves, peeled
3 tablespoons freshly squeezed lemon juice
1 tablespoon tahini
1 teaspoon sea salt
⅓ cup extra-virgin olive oil

1 Place the beans in a small saucepan, cover with water, and soak for 24 hours. Drain the beans, rinse well, and drain again.

2 Transfer the beans to a quart jar and attach a sprouting screen with the jar ring. Prop the jar upside down and at a slight angle over a bowl.

3 Continue to rinse and drain the beans 2 to 3 times a day for the next 2 or 3 days, until the sprouts barely emerge from the beans.

4 Transfer the beans to a clean saucepan and cover them with water. Bring the beans to a boil over medium-high heat, then simmer the beans until tender, about 1 hour. Drain the beans and rinse them under cold water to cool. Drain again.

5 Transfer the beans to a food processor. Add the garlic, lemon juice, tahini, and salt and pulse to combine. Using the feeder tube, add the olive oil in a slow, steady stream with the processor running. Continue to process until the beans and oil are well emulsified. Serve immediately or store in a covered container in the refrigerator and serve chilled.

MAKES 1 PINT

Prep: **5 minutes, plus 5 minutes daily** | Sprouting: **3 to 4 days** | Storage: **5 days**

- -

MAKE IT A MEAL: *Serve hummus with chips for a snack, or spread it on pita and top with falafel for a complete meal. Falafel, deep-fried chickpea patties, taste great with hummus, which provides a smooth, creamy texture to the simple sandwich. Top with cucumbers and red onions, and you have a delicious and nutritious meal full of heart-healthy beans.*

soak them before cooking or other preparations, as this process neutralizes enzyme inhibitors and promotes the growth of digestive enzymes. Before preparing any legumes, grains, or seeds, soak them in cold water. Legumes and seeds should be soaked for 8 to 12 hours, and grains should be soaked for 4 to 8 hours.

Nuts do not sprout, but you can increase their nutritional availability by soaking them before eating. This simple process is helpful in breaking down enzyme inhibitors that can prevent proper digestion. To soak nuts, submerge them in salted water as long as overnight for hard nuts such as almonds, and for just a few hours for softer nuts like cashews, walnuts, and pine nuts. If you normally have any sort of digestive distress after eating nuts, soaking may be the key to alleviating this problem. After the nuts are soaked, they are softened considerably, so they should be dried in a hot, dry skillet or in the oven before eating or using in recipes.

Because these processes are different from fermentation, they will not be covered comprehensively in this book. However, in an effort to introduce you to these companion techniques that can help improve the nutrition you receive from legumes, I've included two recipes using these simple methods. A mere overview of a wide range of skills, these instructions for sprouted grains are easy to get right at home.

WHAT'S NEXT?

So you are ready to get fermenting, but where to start? Sauerkraut is a great launching point. It requires just a few ingredients and no fancy equipment, and it is super easy to ferment to perfection. Unlike other recipes with more variables that can affect success, as long as you follow the directions for making sauerkraut, you are all but guaranteed a great product in the end.

Check out the next chapter to get the basics on items you will need for future projects, such as salt, whey, and other starter cultures, as well as necessary equipment, and then get started with your first ferment. In chapter 3, I will guide you through the process, providing step-by-step instructions along the way. There is also a useful chart to help you determine a few things you can do to improve on your first batch if you feel it needs some work, or if you run into any problems along the way.

Once you try this sauerkraut recipe and believe you've got the process under your belt, select any project from chapters 4 through 9 that interests you, and give it a try. All the recipes in this book are beginner level and perfect for your next fermentation project. Be sure to take lots of notes, so you know what worked and what didn't, and you will be well on your way to fermentation success. Happy fermenting!

FERMENTATION SPOTLIGHT: A NOTE ON WINE AND BEER

 I came to fermentation by way of wine making, and if you are reading this book, you may be interested in making your own wine or beer, too. After all, these are great projects based on the same science and techniques as food ferments, but with entirely different results. They are huge kitchen projects that deserve entire books of their own, and because of this, they aren't covered here, but I want to touch on them a little.

- -

Whether or not you live in a wine-growing or beer-making region, there are plenty of options when it comes to making these brews at home. When I first started making wine, I bought wine-making kits from a nearby home brew store. These kits are very easy to use and will provide you with a perfectly balanced juice that will create a good-tasting wine. Likewise, there are beer-brewing kits with well-balanced ingredients that enable you to brew with success. If you have a home brew shop near you, you'll find plenty of options there, or you can always order these supplies online.

As you become involved in beer or wine making and your interest grows, you can begin to branch out and make beer and wine from local ingredients. These days I purchase grapes from local vineyards, and with the help of a small crew of family, friends, and children, and a smattering of equipment like a crusher/destemmer and press, I make 50 to 100 gallons of wine annually. With a little practice, patience, and research, you too can brew like a master in no time.

There are many books that offer extremely comprehensive information on beer and wine making. If you are interested in beginning your own brewing or wine-making operation in your home, I urge you to check out the Resources at the back of this book (page 219) for some great books on these enormously fun crafts.

CHAPTER TWO

The Starter Kitchen

There is no shortage of companies selling high-end fermentation equipment. And the truth is that some of the supplies are very tempting. But don't let a lack of funds or fancy equipment prevent you from getting involved in fermentation. Sure, hand-crafted ceramic fermentation vessels are nice, especially if you decide you want to make a huge batch of pickles or sauerkraut, but in reality you can get started with just a few simple items.

ESSENTIAL EQUIPMENT

The bare-bones basics you need to get started are set out for you below. Make sure you have these, and you'll be ready to begin your first project.

Fermentation Vessel

The most important item you will need is a fermentation vessel. If you are just starting out, it's easiest to use a mason jar. Quart jars will work, although a half-gallon jar makes things a bit simpler and lets you make larger batches. These can both be found anywhere canning supplies are sold, as well as online. Try to find jars with a wide mouth.

Once you get started and find that you enjoy fermenting, you may want to increase production. In this case, a ceramic pickling crock is a great investment. Ohio Stoneware offers American-made crocks in sizes ranging from ½ gallon to 6 gallons for reasonable prices. I have several that I've collected over the years in varying sizes, and I love them, especially for large batches of pickles or sauerkraut.

In lieu of a fermentation crock or mason jars, any container made of food-safe glass, food-safe ceramic, or food-safe plastic will work.

Weights

Weights are used during lacto-fermentation to create an anaerobic environment, meaning an environment where the food is not exposed to oxygen. Weights can be anything from rocks to shot glasses to votive candleholders to narrow-mouth mason jars to

EQUIPMENT YOU DON'T NEED

Specialty Fermenting Jars: Some people swear by the various fermenting jars with airlocks that create an anaerobic environment. While these jars are nice, they are by no means necessary. You are creating an anaerobic environment when you submerge produce in its brine, regardless of whether or not you trap all the oxygen out of the jar with an airlock. If you have some extra cash, go ahead and try one, but know that these are not necessary for fermenting, no matter what other people tell you.

Specialty Fermenting Vessels: I am always drawn to beautiful stoneware, and there is no shortage of handmade vessels designed for fermenting. While they look lovely and are practical, often with an inner lip to hold ferments below the brine, they come with a hefty price tag and are certainly not necessary, especially when you are first starting out.

food-safe resealable bags filled with brine. The main factor is that they are cleaned thoroughly before using. For rocks, this means scrubbing them in soapy water and then boiling for 10 minutes. Other items can be washed well and left to air-dry before using.

Utensils

You will need some utensils for working with your ferments. A jar filler or funnel is a great tool to have on hand, especially if you will be fermenting in mason jars. This is an inexpensive tool available anywhere canning supplies are sold. You will also need a variety of nonreactive spoons and/or forks for working with your ferments. Stainless steel is fine, but bamboo or food-safe plastic are better options. Finally, a strainer will be necessary if you are making kefir or water kefir.

Scale

While not 100 percent necessary, a kitchen scale is highly recommended and a great tool to have in your kitchen. Many of the recipes in this book use weight as a measurement instead of volume because it is more accurate. Kitchen scales are relatively inexpensive (under $20) and can prevent some serious inaccuracy in the kitchen. If you don't have one, you can always weigh produce at the market, but if you plan on fermenting regularly, a scale will definitely be worth the investment. Ideally, you should weigh produce after preparing it—this means, for instance, that cabbage should be weighed after it has been cored, which can pose a

problem if you are relying on the scale at the grocery store.

Containers

Nonreactive, sturdy, and attractive, mason jars are the go-to option for storing most types of ferments. You can choose from a variety of styles and sizes to store all your different recipes. Plus, their airtight lids also make them perfect for storing dry items in your pantry. If you have already begun fermenting, you likely have several on hand; if not, any Pyrex containers with lids can be used, as well as any food-safe plastic storage containers.

Lids

Investing in a box of plastic mason jar lids is a great idea when you begin fermenting. They are available online or anywhere canning supplies are sold. If you don't have access to these or would rather do without, use regular two-piece canning jar lids lined with a layer of plastic wrap between the ferment and the lid.

Bottles

For kombucha and mead, swing-top bottles are your best option. If you live near a home brew store, you can pick up a case of bottles and save on shipping costs. Alternatively, save some old Grolsch beer bottles (or any other flip-top type), and repurpose them for your fermenting projects. You will also need a bottle brush to clean swing-top bottles and remove stuck-on particles.

THE INGREDIENTS

Salt

Salt is the cornerstone of many of the ferments in the book. It is used to make dill pickles, kimchi, sauerkraut, and many lesser-known types of vegetable and fruit ferments. Salt is not actually a starter culture, but it inhibits the growth of pathogenic bacteria, allowing for the friendly bacteria to thrive. Pickling and canning salt or sea salt can be used for fermentation, as can kosher salt. The recipes in this book typically call for pickling and canning salt because the grain is smaller, allowing it to dissolve easily in water without heat. Kosher salt works, too, although you will likely have to heat and then cool the brine before using. You may also substitute sea salt, but avoid any colored sea salts or those containing anti-caking agents.

Water

Water is used in most ferments where a brine is not created naturally, such as pickles, carrots, some kimchi recipes, fruit ferments, grain ferments, and most beverages. It is important that this water is free of fluoride and chlorine, as these can impair fermentation. Tap water is generally fine if its flavor is good. If not, choose distilled water.

If your tap water is chlorinated, let it stand in a large jar at room temperature for 12 to 24 hours to eliminate the chlorine before proceeding. Alternatively, you can boil the water for 1 to 2 minutes and then let it cool.

Whey

Whey is used in fruit ferments, a few vegetable ferments, grain ferments, and some beverages such as beet kvass. Simply put, it is the liquid that remains after milk has been curdled, but you can also get whey from low and whole fat yogurt and kefir. For more information on how to make whey, see page 31. For those who are lactose intolerant, whey is not a good choice. In this case, another pickling brine or kombucha can be used as a starter culture. People who merely have a dairy sensitivity may be able to use whey without negative effect.

Starter Cultures

For some recipes in this book, liquids such as kombucha or pickling brine can be used in place of salt; if you prefer, you can also use dried starter cultures, such as Caldwell's Starter Culture. While there are no specific recipes in this book using commercial cultures, they are a viable option, especially if you want to cut down on sodium in your diet. To use these cultures, adjust the recipes here by following the package directions on the product.

Recipes for which you'll need a starter culture include kefir, kombucha, and yogurt; you can also use a starter culture for some vegetable ferments, if you like. Kefir requires kefir grains, which are small cottage cheese–looking curds, and kombucha requires a SCOBY, or symbiotic culture of bacteria and yeast. These can be purchased from the sources listed in the back of this book (see page 219), or if you know someone who makes either of these at home, I urge you to inquire about getting some extra from them. These are both self-replicating cultures that continue to grow as you make kefir and kombucha, so once you buy one, you are set—chances are, after not too long, you will even have some extra.

To make your own yogurt, you can use a couple of tablespoons of yogurt from a commercial batch. The key is to find a brand that contains live cultures, which will be stated on the label. Many such varieties of yogurt are available, and you should be able to find one at your local supermarket. For the best results, choose one that is plain (unflavored), with no added sugars or thickening agents.

Apple Cider Vinegar

Apple cider vinegar can be used to start other vinegar ferments and is one of the main ingredients of drinking shrubs. But don't reach for the gallon jug at the supermarket. For fermentation, you will need raw (unpasteurized) vinegar. This can be found at many well-stocked grocery stores, as well as specialty markets. The most commonly available brand is Bragg, but be on the lookout for others as well. In the case of Bragg, the "mother," or fermenting bacteria, is still in the jar and creates a murky appearance in the vinegar. This is completely normal and not a sign of spoilage.

Honey

Honey is used in some ferments to add sweetness. However, this is not the honey typically available at the grocery store. For these recipes, you will need raw (unpasteurized) honey, which you can find seasonally at farmers' markets or at specialty stores. This is the only type of honey that should be used for fermenting.

FAQ How Do You Make Whey?

Whey can easily be separated from homemade yogurt and kefir, as well as from plain yogurt or kefir purchased from the store. If you are purchasing yogurt or kefir from the store to strain the whey, make sure to read the label first and confirm that the product contains live cultures, as these are vital for whey to work in fermentation. While the cheese-making process also creates whey, this whey cannot be used for future ferments, as the milk in this case is typically heated above the point at which beneficial bacteria can live.

To begin the process, place a funnel over a mason jar. Line a mesh strainer with a couple of coffee filters and place the strainer over the funnel. Pour the kefir or yogurt into the strainer and let the whey drain off from the curds. When complete, place a lid on the jar, label it with the date, and store the whey in your refrigerator, where it will keep for at least 2 weeks. Consider making Kefir Cheese (page 131) with that strainer full of curds!

Produce

Fresh produce is important for fermentation. Bruises and cracks in the skin of produce can give way to mold and spoilage, so selecting the best is important. While some fresh items, like daikon, can wait several days before fermenting, others such as cucumbers should not. Look at individual recipes for special tips regarding storing and using certain fruits and vegetables before beginning any project. This book uses predominately fresh produce, but some foods such as jams or syrups, where texture is not an issue, can be made from frozen produce as well.

Purchasing organic produce is another issue to which you should give some thought before beginning any fermentation project. For foods to be certified organic by the USDA, the farmers must adhere to certain standards for fertilizers, pesticides, and herbicides applied to the foods. However, this certification requires farmers to pay a fee to licensing agencies, a task that is often not possible for smaller farms. One way to avoid paying higher prices and still get quality produce is to shop at your local farmers' market, where you can speak directly to the farmers and learn their farming practices. Just because a farm is not certified organic does not mean it should be ruled out: the only way to know for sure is to talk to the people growing the food.

Purchasing organic foods is important for fermentation because it ensures that there is plenty of naturally occurring bacteria on the surface of the fruits and vegetables. However, it is especially important to buy organic when you will be eating the rind or peel of the produce, where the most pesticide residue is typically concentrated. This category includes cucumbers, apples, and grapes, among others.

In addition, before starting any project in this book, be sure to consult the Dirty Dozen and Clean Fifteen lists in the appendix of this book (page 215). These lists are compiled annually by the Environmental Working Group. The Dirty Dozen lists the 12 most pesticide-contaminated crops, which are those you should always avoid buying conventionally farmed. Buy organic when it comes to these fruits and vegetables; if that isn't possible, avoid that produce altogether. On the other side of the spectrum, the Clean Fifteen highlights 15 foods that are minimally sprayed, if at all, throughout the growing season, making them safe to buy through conventional sources.

SHOPPING FOR FIVE FERMENTS

In the following section I have outlined how to shop for five basic ferments. Use these simple tips to help guide you in selecting the best produce to get your fermenting projects underway with ease.

Dill Pickles
(page 51)

When making pickles, you need cucumbers that are 3 to 5 inches long. Don't be tempted to buy larger ones, thinking they will produce better pickles. For fermentation you always want to stick with smaller cucumbers, and be sure to choose true pickling cucumbers. In many stores, I have seen what are labeled as mini (or Persian) cucumbers for eating fresh, but these are not the same as pickling cucumbers, which have a thicker, slightly bitter skin. Select cucumbers that are firm and free of bruises and blemishes. Because they must be used within 1 or 2 days from picking, be sure to buy the cucumbers right before you intend to begin a project.

Strawberry-Mint Chia Jam (page 101)

Strawberries are on the Dirty Dozen list, so you will want to find organic options. Like cucumbers, strawberries are very prone to spoilage, so be sure to purchase them only about a day before beginning your fermenting project. If possible, procure strawberries from a local source. Many varieties of strawberries, such as those grown locally, are not sold in stores because they do not last long fresh. Unlike commercial varieties that are engineered to hold up well during transport—and subsequently taste like cardboard—local varieties are usually bursting with flavor. Buy these from farm stands, or pick them yourself at a u-pick field.

Mint can be purchased at a grocery store, or you can grow it yourself rather easily. Store it with its cut ends in a glass of water.

Orange-Spiced Kefir (page 129)

For kefir, the higher-quality milk you start out with, the better the finished product will be. Always choose milk that is pasteurized

IN A PICKLE

When most people think of pickles, it's cucumber pickles that come to mind. However, there is a wide world of pickles out there, and cucumbers are just a small minority. While there are a few cucumber pickle recipes in this book, you'll notice a lot of attention paid to many lesser-known pickles, too, since the fact is that cucumber pickles can be quite finicky. You can produce a great batch one day, and a not-so-great batch the next, while other pickles are much easier to get right each and every time.

In this book, you'll find a focus on cabbage, which is quite uncomplicated to ferment into numerous variations of sauerkraut and kimchi. Beyond that, you can easily preserve carrots, cauliflower, beets, beans, and nearly all garden produce through pickling, so I've included a wide range here—not to mention the whole category of relishes, chutneys, and salsas, sweet and savory combinations that are simple to ferment with success the first time.

(in the refrigerated dairy aisle) rather than ultra-pasteurized (usually unrefrigerated, in aseptic containers). Select organic milk whenever possible. At the very least, seek out milk that does not include artificial growth hormones (rSBT or rBGH). In the United States, this is stated on the label. Milk from cows that graze on grass is preferred to milk from cows that eat grain, as it contains higher concentrations of vitamins A, D, E, and K_2. If raw milk is an option for you, this can also work.

Because you are using the whole orange for this recipe, including the peel, it is best to source organic oranges.

Lacto-Fermented Peach Chutney (page 182)

Peaches are also on the Dirty Dozen list, so choosing organic is a good idea. Whether picking peaches yourself or buying them at the store, select ones that are slightly under-ripe, and allow them to ripen at room temperature at home. You can make this recipe when the peaches are still slightly underripe to make their skin removal easier.

Ginger-Pear Kombucha (page 199)

Select pears that are organic, as you are using the whole pear, peel and all. Pick whichever type of pear is your favorite, or select one that is in season and at a good price. Because pears bruise easily, handle them carefully, store them in the refrigerator, and cut off any bruised spots before using.

Ginger can contain high levels of pesticides when grown conventionally. This does not pose a large problem when you eat small amounts, but if you regularly drink a ginger-kombucha blend or use it for therapeutic purposes, select organic ginger.

THE ENVIRONMENT

One of the most important factors that can affect the outcomes of all types of ferments is the environment in which they are created. This includes everything from the containers in which you ferment to the place where your ferments are kept. Factors such as contamination, heat, and sunlight all play roles in the outcome of any project, and taking these items into account can make the difference between success and failure.

Sanitization

This includes the containers you use for fermenting, as well as the space in which you prepare your ferment. As with any type of cooking, you want to avoid cross-contamination, so be sure to keep cutting boards used for meat, fish, and poultry separate from those used for vegetables and fruit. Thoroughly clean and sanitize all surfaces, cutting boards, and utensils, preferably with warm soapy water followed by a mixture of vinegar and water for sanitization.

Your hands should also be kept clean, but avoid the use of antibacterial soaps, which can have a negative effect on ferments. Jars should be impeccably clean when beginning a project.

In some cases, the instructions will say to use sanitized jars, particularly in the case of ferments more prone to spoilage or those that ferment for a long time. In this case, simply boil the jar in water for 10 minutes before using to kill any present mold or bacteria.

Temperature

In the winter, fermenting in your kitchen may be a good idea, as the kitchen generally remains warmer than the rest of the house. Most ferments do best at around 72°F, though there is some variation to this, with the most successful sauerkraut fermented at around 65°F. For cooler ferments, a root cellar, basement, or other cooler spot is ideal, though not altogether necessary. However, avoiding the kitchen during summer months is almost always necessary, as temperatures can spike considerably while cooking. Choose a spot that maintains a steady temperature throughout the day for best results.

Sunlight

Sunlight should be avoided for all ferments, as it can heat things up too high, leading to spoilage and way-too-quick fermentation. Choose a spot that is out of direct sunlight— and perhaps even dark, if possible. I sometimes ferment things in the cupboard, as it stays dark and cool. However, if you are going to do this, make sure to check on things periodically, as you don't want any forgotten jars exploding due to excessive gas buildup!

CHAPTER 3

Sauerkraut

YOUR FIRST FERMENT

Sauerkraut may not seem glamorous, but unless you have experienced the homemade variety, chances are you have never tasted the nuanced flavors of this authentic fermented product. Bursting with personality, sauerkraut is perhaps one of the easiest ferments to make at home and get right the first time. And once you get these basics down, you can use this knowledge to build your confidence and try your hand at more complex recipes.

DON'T SKIP THIS CHAPTER!

Even if you are convinced that you don't like sauerkraut, check out this chapter anyway. It has lots of information that can be applicable to any fruit or vegetable fermentation project. It's a great primer to get you started—and who knows, you may end up liking sauerkraut after all!

The following steps of sauerkraut making apply to other fermentation projects:

- Getting your work area ready for fermentation
- Prepping vegetables using a knife and cutting board
- Weighing and measuring ingredients
- Salting vegetables for fermentation
- Packing vegetables into a fermentation vessel, and properly weighting them down
- Storing fermenting vegetables
- Judging the doneness of fermented vegetables
- Troubleshooting problems with fermented vegetables

BEFORE YOU GET STARTED

Before beginning any fermenting project, there are several steps you should complete to improve your chances for success. Once you tackle a few projects following these steps, they will become a regular part of your fermenting routine.

Fermenting is a low-tech process that can be done in any clean kitchen using basic equipment. When starting out, set reasonable goals and gain confidence as you go by completing successful projects. For even more fun, ferment with friends. You are more than welcome to ferment alone, but it is exponentially more fun to chop loads of vegetables or fruit while in good company—and maybe with a nice glass of wine.

Prep Your Equipment

All jars, fermentation vessels, and utensils should be washed in hot, soapy water before beginning. Rinse them well, and then sanitize them with a commercial or homemade sanitizer. To make a sanitizing solution, mix 1 tablespoon of bleach into 2 quarts of water. Dip each item in this solution, rinse it in cool water, and allow it to air-dry. Alternatively, you can use commercial vinegar to sanitize, or run the items through the dishwasher prior to use.

Keep It Clean

Wash your hands thoroughly before beginning, using a soap that is not antibacterial. Wipe down all work surfaces with a bleach-water solution, vinegar, or commercial sanitizer before beginning. Keep utensils and other items that you are using on a clean surface such as a baking sheet as you work to prevent contamination. Focus on only one project at a time, completing it in its entirety before moving on to something new.

Arrange Your Mise en Place

As with cooking, it is important to lay out your fermenting ingredients and supplies before you begin a project. Fermenting requires a high level of cleanliness, and gathering everything first ensures that you will not be touching and contaminating items used for preservation during the preparation period.

Take Notes

One of the most valuable things that you can do to help fine-tune your fermenting skills is take notes. Otherwise, you will forget many details worth correcting in the future, and the next time you'll be right back where you started. Recording your observations, successes, and failures is a great way to enhance your skills, which is why every recipe in this book gives you space for notes.

Equipment

Bowl	Kitchen towel
Kitchen scale	Quart jar
Knife	Shot glass
Cutting board	Jar lid and ring
Measuring spoons	

SAUERKRAUT AROUND THE WORLD

The word *sauerkraut* comes from Germany, and it is no secret that sauerkraut is a specialty in that country. However, it is also popular throughout much of Europe. Its high vitamin C content prevented scurvy for sailors on long journeys in olden times, and its mildly laxative properties have been hailed throughout the centuries, especially in winter when fresh produce was hard to come by.

The Asian equivalent of sauerkraut, kimchi, has been fermented in Korea for centuries. However, it was not until the late 1500s that kimchi took on its present-day spicy form, when the red chile was introduced through European contact. Prior to that, it was similar to salted cabbage, fueling the age-old question: Where did sauerkraut originally come from?

Some of the oldest references to sauerkraut date back to ancient Rome, while variations with carrots and turnips have origins in Russia, Ukraine, and Belarus. Other sources say that Chinese laborers ate sauerkraut during the construction of the Great Wall of China, with Genghis Khan later introducing the fermented food to Europe in the late twelfth century.

No matter when it may have originated, some variation of sausage and sauerkraut is served now in most European countries. Sauerkraut production became popular in Europe in the early seventeenth century, and nearly 100 years later, German immigrants brought it to America, where the craft continues to flourish today.

SAUERKRAUT
TROUBLESHOOTING TIPS

Sauerkraut is a great place to start fermenting because it is fairly easy to get right the first time. However, there is always the chance that something can run amok. When a problem does occur, identifying and remedying it quickly is the best way to save your ferment. In some cases, you may have to toss it, but keeping a vigilant eye on the fermenting kraut and following the directions correctly will prevent most mishaps.

PROBLEM	CAUSE	SOLUTION
Scum on top	Scum is caused by yeast. Be sure to weight down the sauerkraut sufficiently to prevent scum growth.	Skim off scum daily and continue fermenting.
Mold on top	Mold often occurs when the temperature is too high, or the kraut was not well covered in brine.	Remove moldy kraut and continue fermenting.
Darkened on top	Sauerkraut darkens as a result of oxidation, which is caused by uneven salting, poor storage, or high fermentation temperatures.	Discard darkened kraut and continue fermenting.
Pink on top	A pink color is the result of a yeast overgrowth. This is caused by poor weighting, inadequate covering, or too much salt.	Remove pink kraut and continue fermenting.
Sliminess	Sliminess can be caused by high fermentation temperatures or too little salt.	Dump the entire batch. Sliminess is always a sign of spoilage, and any ferment that is slimy should be thrown away.

BASIC SAUERKRAUT

MAKES 1 QUART

Prep: **10 minutes** | Rest: **30 minutes** | Fermentation: **2 to 6 weeks** | Storage: **6 weeks**

- -

Sauerkraut has a storied past, dating back to the ancient Romans. Eaten by sailors for centuries to ward off scurvy during prolonged trips across the oceans, this simple ferment has long held a place in global food history. Cultures throughout the world have developed their own versions, and this is the basic building block for many other ferments. This is the most basic kind of sauerkraut you can make, and a great place to start ferment-ing. With just salt and cabbage, you create a delicious ferment that can be stuffed into a sandwich or eaten by the forkful. Don't let its minimalist style have you thinking that it is in any way subpar. This plain sauerkraut has a mellow, almost buttery flavor when fermented to perfec-tion. If you like, you can add 1 teaspoon of dill seeds, caraway seeds, or juniper berries to your ferment to enhance the flavor even further.

**2 or 3 green or red cabbage heads
 (enough to yield 2 pounds cored,
 shredded cabbage)**
4 teaspoons pickling salt

1 Remove the outermost leaves from the cabbage and throw them away. Using a sharp knife, cut the cabbage in half, and then cut each half into quarters. From each quarter, cut away the core. Hold the cabbage firmly as you work with it, placing the flat sides down to prevent rolling and slipping. Working with one section at a time, cut the cabbage into thin, long slices, between ⅛ and ¼ inch thick. The thicker you slice the cabbage, the crunchier it will be after fermentation. When the cabbage pieces become too small to slice easily, turn or flip them as needed to make them stable on the cutting board.

Place a bowl on your kitchen scale, and zero out the weight so that you are able to determine the exact weight of the cabbage. Transfer the cabbage to the bowl until you have 2 pounds.

continues ►

2   Add the salt to the cabbage. Working with clean hands, mix and firmly massage the salt into the cabbage. Fresh cabbage will begin to release liquid almost immediately, while older cabbage may take several minutes. Once the salt is well dispersed, cover the bowl with a clean kitchen towel and set it aside at room temperature for 30 minutes. During this time, it will release a lot of water, and a brine will begin to form.

3   Pack the cabbage into a quart jar, firmly pressing it down as you go. Your fist works well for this, as does a small jar that will fit inside your fermentation vessel. Pour any juices from the bowl into the jar. Press out as much air as possible, leaving about 1 inch of headspace at the top of the jar. By the time you get all the cabbage packed into the jar, the liquid should have risen above the cabbage.

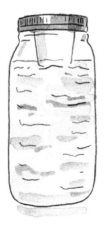

4   Use a shot glass or other weight to hold the cabbage down below the brine. Affix a lid to the jar and place the jar in a cool, dark location. Sauerkraut works best between 50° and 75°F, where it will ferment slowly and develop the most nuanced flavor.

5 About 24 hours after you pack the cabbage into the jar, the brine should be completely covering the cabbage. If not, make a brine solution by dissolving 1 teaspoon pickling salt in 1 cup water, and add this as needed to the jar to submerge the cabbage.

6 Check in on your sauerkraut every day or two, always taking note of the liquid level and ensuring that the cabbage stays beneath it. After a few days, you will notice bubbles forming and rising to the surface, signaling that fermentation is taking place. From that point on, every couple of days you will need to remember to loosen the lid and "burp" out any trapped gases, then tighten it up again. Depending on the temperature of the room where fermentation is occurring, bubbles may stop rising anywhere from 2 to 6 weeks after the start of fermentation, signaling that the process is complete. However, you can eat the sauerkraut anytime you like from early to late in the fermentation process. Try tasting the sauerkraut periodically, using a clean utensil to remove a sample after 2 weeks to see what you think.

When you are satisfied with the flavor, transfer the jar to the refrigerator.

Notes:

A CLOSER LOOK: *To get the probiotic benefits of sauerkraut, it must be eaten raw, as heating it to any temperature above 115°F inactivates the living bacteria and yeasts it contains. However, this does not mean you should never cook with sauerkraut, as cooking gives it a slightly different but equally delicious flavor. Try it both raw and cooked, and see what you think.*

FERMENTING TROUBLESHOOTING GUIDE

As with any kitchen project, sometimes things go wrong. The good thing is that problems with ferments are relatively easy to identify. For all ferments, you should follow the assessments below before eating.

Visible Assessment

Bubbles are a sign that fermentation is taking place, and are completely normal to see during this process. If you come from the canning world, you may be leery of this, as you are trained not to eat things that are bubbling. In the world of fermenting, though, this is exactly what we are after.

Once the fermentation gets underway, you may see what looks like foam or scum on the surface of the ferment. This is completely normal, too, although it should be removed on a daily basis by simply skimming it off with a clean utensil.

Throughout fermentation, the amount of brine may rise as the liquid in fruits or vegetables is extracted. This, too, is completely standard. You may want to place a small plate under fermenting jars to prevent spills during the active fermentation period.

The color and texture of many fruits and vegetables change significantly during fermentation. This is to be expected.

Smell

If you are new to fermenting, you may find some of the aromas strange and sometimes even unpleasant. However, fermented foods should never smell putrid or rotten. If they do, something has gone wrong and they should be tossed out.

Taste

Fermented foods should taste good. While some of these flavors and tastes may be new to you, fermented foods should not taste bad. If something does end up tasting bad, discard it.

FAQ What Can I Use to Weight Down Vegetables under the Brine?

When fermenting in a quart jar, the easiest thing to use as a weight to hold vegetables below the brine is a clean half-pint or jelly jar. These jars fit easily into the mouth of a wide-mouth quart jar and can be filled with water to weight the vegetables down. Other objects that work well are shot glasses and small glass weights specifically designed for fermentation. Cleaned and boiled rocks can also be used for this purpose.

Part 2 The Recipes

CHAPTER FOUR

Vegetables

Cucumber pickles may be the first thing that comes to mind when you think of fermented vegetables, but the truth is that just about any vegetable can be cultured. This age-old technique to preserve the harvest is a great place to start your fermenting journey. Vegetables are notoriously easy to ferment, and your options are about as wide as your imagination.

Brassicas, such as cabbage, radishes, cauliflower, kohlrabi, and turnips, are some of the best fermenters, while carrots, cucumbers, parsnips, beets, beans, and celery can be a bit trickier. Jump-start your fermenting hobby with these introductory vegetable ferments, which span the globe in flavor, technique, and tradition.

Recipes

VEGETABLE FERMENTATION BASICS

Every ferment is different, but these vegetable fermentation basics can help you gauge the overall process and set you on your way.

Getting Prepared

• **Prep your ingredients before you get started.** Fermentation times are based on the preparation method outlined in each recipe. If you make changes to this, you will need to adjust fermentation times accordingly. Larger pieces require more fermentation time, while smaller cuts require less fermentation time.

• **Swap out produce when desired.** If you prefer napa cabbage or red cabbage to green cabbage, go for it. If you like a different type of root vegetable or brassica, it is your choice to make that switch. The result will be different, but you have control. The only caveat to this is vegetables that cannot be eaten raw, such as potatoes.

• **Keep ratios in mind.** Most important to keep in mind is the ratio of salt or other starter culture to water. You can play around with produce types, spices, and herbs, but adhere to these proportions, as they are what protect your food during fermentation.

The Fermentation Process

• **Weight vegetables down below the brine.** Vegetable ferments require an anaerobic environment, which is achieved by keeping vegetables below the brine, limiting their exposure to oxygen.

• **Keep the vegetables covered.** If for any reason the vegetables are not covered by brine, create some additional brine to do so. Dissolve 1 tablespoon pickling salt in 1 cup water, and pour this over the vegetables.

• **Release gases.** It is important that you "burp" the jar every few days to allow built-up gases to escape. This is done by simply loosening the lid until you hear the gases release, then tightening it up again.

• **Sample your ferment.** The fermentation times in this book are accurate, but personal preference and your fermenting environment play a role as well. Taste often, using a clean utensil when removing food from jars. When you are satisfied with the flavor, cap it with a lid and place it in the refrigerator to halt fermentation.

Vegetables

VEGETABLE
TROUBLESHOOTING TIPS

Too salty. If a ferment is complete but tastes too salty, try rinsing or even soaking the vegetables in fresh water before serving to remove some of the salt. Alternatively, add a little water to the jar to dilute the brine, and give the vegetables a good stir.

Not fermenting. It typically takes 2 to 3 days for fermentation to get underway. However, temperature has a lot to do with it. If 3 days have passed and you haven't seen any bubbles, try moving the jar to a slightly warmer location. This will likely not be an issue in the summer, but in cold winter months you might need to place ferments in the kitchen or another warmer room for fermentation to get started.

Scum. While it may look disturbing, this is actually a pretty normal occurrence when fermenting and not a problem if taken care of in a timely manner. Check ferments daily or every other day for scum, and skim it off the surface when it appears. Be sure to rinse off the weights as well.

Foul smell. Pickled vegetables smell strongly, and to some people, the smell is not pleasant. However, they should not smell foul or putrid. If they do, toss them.

Mold on top. If mold begins to grow on the surface of the vegetables, chances are they are not properly weighted down or were old when you got them. In most cases, you can remove the mold and continue, especially when making sauerkraut or other shredded ferments where a layer can be easily removed. If the mold looks fuzzy or appears extensive, however, discard the ferment.

Smells like alcohol. Though unlikely, it is possible for a vegetable ferment to become alcoholic, especially if the vegetables you are using are high in sugar. This is not desirable, so if your ferment begins to smell alcoholic, you need to toss the ferment out.

starter recipe DILL PICKLES

MAKES 1 QUART   Prep: **10 minutes** | Fermentation: **1 to 4 weeks** | Storage: **1 to 2 months**

An expertly made dill pickle is something to behold, balancing equal parts acidic funk and the soothing flavor of dill. The recipe yields 1 quart, but feel free to double, triple, or quadruple it based on your love of pickles. Start small and work your way up as you become comfortable with the process. For best results, use freshly picked 3- to 5-inch pickling cucumbers. The high tannin content of the grape leaves helps keep the pickles crisp—if you have them, use them. If not, don't let it stop you, as you can still create tasty pickles without them.

1¼ pounds pickling cucumbers
2 grape leaves (optional)
1 dill head
1 small red onion, cut into wedges
5 garlic cloves, peeled and smashed with the back of a knife
1 dried chile, slit lengthwise
5 black peppercorns
1¾ tablespoons pickling salt
2½ cups water

1   Clean the cucumbers well under cold water. Remove the blossom ends with a knife.

2   In a quart jar, combine the grape leaves (if using), dill, onion, garlic, chile, and peppercorns. Pack the cucumbers tightly into the jar.

continues ▶

3 In a small bowl, dissolve the salt in the water, and pour this brine over the cucumbers.

4 Make sure that the cucumbers are completely submerged in the brine. If necessary, use a weight to hold the cucumbers down.

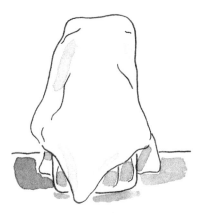

5 Cover the jar with a clean kitchen towel and set aside at room temperature.

6 After 2 or 3 days, fermentation will have started, and bubbles will begin rising to the surface. Remove any scum that forms on the surface daily, and make sure that the cucumbers remain submerged below the brine.

7 When the bubbles stop rising, fermentation is complete; however, you may begin tasting the pickles after about a week. When they taste good to you, cap the jar with a nonreactive lid and transfer to the refrigerator to halt fermentation.

Notes:

PREP TIP: *If you don't have access to grape leaves, sour cherry and oak leaves both produce the same effect. Because of their high tannin content, all these leaves can help pickles stay crisp during fermentation and maintain their bright green color.*

CUCUMBER PICKLE
TROUBLESHOOTING TIPS

The first time I made dill pickles, they were a mess. Way too salty, the pickles were nearly unpalatable without a serious soak in water. Over the years, my pickling skills have definitely improved, and I have created many, many successful batches, so don't let early failures stop you from proceeding. Even though cucumbers are one of the most common pickles, they can be tricky to ferment well. Check out some of these basic troubleshooting tips to ensure your pickles turn out great.

- -

Hollow middles. This problem typically lies in one of two areas: the watering stage while cucumbers are maturing, or the processing stage before cucumbers become pickles. If you are growing your own cucumbers, be sure to water the plants well, especially once cucumbers develop. If you are purchasing cucumbers, buy from a quality farm that you trust. Then remember that cucumbers should be processed within 48 hours of picking for the best results. Also, keep in mind that while hollow pickles will not win any beauty contests, they are still completely edible.

- -

Shriveled, soft pickles. This occurs when cucumbers are stored too long before processing. To prevent this from occurring, be sure to purchase from a farm you trust, and ask when the cucumbers were picked. As stated above, cucumbers should be processed within 48 hours of picking.

- -

Off flavors. Bad flavors in your pickles can result from the growth of undesirable microbes during fermentation. However, as long as the pickles are not slimy or moldy, they are fine to eat. In future batches, ensure that the salt content is adequate, that you trim the blossom ends of the cucumbers, and that you skim the brine regularly.

- -

Slimy pickles. Whenever sliminess occurs, it is a sign of spoilage. Ferments become slimy when undesirable microbes grow during fermentation. This can occur for all the same reasons listed for off flavors. The difference is that once pickles reach this stage, they are not safe to eat. Discard the entire batch, clean your fermentation vessel well, and start again.

FIRE KRAUT

Garlic, ginger, and red pepper flakes give this sauerkraut its bite, and create a good balance of spicy and savory appeal. In my family, this gets eaten pretty quickly on its own, but if you have the chance, try making sausage and sauerkraut with this spicy blend to kick it up a notch. If you want it even hotter, seek out Thai chiles.

2 or 3 green cabbage heads (enough to yield 2 pounds cored, shredded cabbage)

6 garlic cloves, peeled and smashed with the back of a knife

1 tablespoon red pepper flakes

1 (1-inch) piece ginger, peeled and cut into matchsticks

4 teaspoons pickling salt

1 Remove the outer leaves from the cabbage and discard. Halve and then quarter the cabbage, and cut the core from each piece. With the cut side down, slice the cabbage into thin strips between ⅛ and ¼ inch thick.

2 Combine the cabbage, garlic, red pepper flakes, ginger, and pickling salt in a large bowl. With clean hands, mix the ingredients, massaging the salt into the cabbage. Cover the bowl with a clean kitchen towel and leave to rest at room temperature for 30 minutes.

3 Pack the cabbage mixture into a quart jar, pressing down firmly as you go. Pour any remaining juices from the bowl into the jar to cover the mixture. Use a weight to hold the cabbage below the brine. Cover the jar with a lid and place in a cool location.

4 After 2 or 3 days, fermentation will have started. Check the sauerkraut every day or two, loosening the lid to "burp" out any trapped gases and remove any scum that forms on the surface. Always make sure that the kraut is submerged below the brine. Re-weight the kraut, close the lid, and continue to monitor its progress. After 2 weeks, taste the kraut. At this time, it will still be quite crunchy and only lightly fermented. If you like it, transfer it to the refrigerator to halt fermentation. If you are not yet satisfied with the flavor, replace the lid and continue to ferment for up to 6 weeks, tasting regularly. Transfer it to the refrigerator once it's done.

MAKES 1 QUART

Prep: **10 minutes** | Rest: **30 minutes** | Fermentation: **2 to 6 weeks** | Storage: **6 weeks**

Notes:

SAUERKRAUT WITH CARROTS

At least to my taste buds, carrots make a perfect addition to sauerkraut, as they lend a wonderful texture that livens up the ferment. I prefer them in discs to create plenty of crunch, even after a long fermentation, but feel free to shred them with the cabbage if you prefer a more uniformly balanced bite to your sauerkraut. Packed with beta-carotene, carrots tremendously enhance the nutritional benefits of your kraut.

2 green cabbage heads (enough to yield 1½ pounds cored, shredded cabbage)

3 carrots, sliced

4 teaspoons pickling salt

1 Remove the outer leaves from the cabbage and discard. Halve and then quarter the cabbage, and cut the core from each piece. With the cut side down, slice the cabbage into thin strips between ⅛ and ¼ inch thick.

2 Combine the cabbage, carrots, and pickling salt in a large bowl. With clean hands, mix the ingredients, massaging the salt into the cabbage. Cover the bowl with a clean kitchen towel and leave to rest at room temperature for 30 minutes.

3 Pack the cabbage mixture into a quart jar, pressing down firmly as you go. Pour any remaining juices from the bowl into the jar to cover the mixture. Use a weight to hold the cabbage mixture below the brine. Cover the jar with a lid and place in a cool location.

4 After 2 or 3 days, fermentation will have started. Check the sauerkraut every day or two, loosening the lid to "burp" out trapped gases and remove any scum that forms on the surface. Always make sure that the kraut is submerged below the brine. Re-weight the kraut, close the lid, and continue to monitor its progress. After 2 weeks, taste the kraut. At this time, it will still be crunchy and only lightly fermented. If you like it, transfer it to the refrigerator to halt fermentation. If you are not yet satisfied, replace the lid and continue to ferment for up to 6 weeks, tasting regularly. Transfer it to the refrigerator once it's done.

MAKES 1 QUART

Prep: **15 minutes** | Rest: **30 minutes** | Fermentation: **2 to 6 weeks** | Storage: **6 weeks**

- -

Notes:

- -

PREP TIP: *There's no need to peel the carrots for this recipe, as their skin has plenty of beneficial bacteria on it. Choose organic carrots if possible, and scrub them clean to remove any dirt or residue.*

CURTIDO

Latin America's version of sauerkraut is crisp, spicy, and vinegary. A short fermentation time leaves the cabbage much firmer than a typical sauerkraut, and the jalapeños and pepper flakes give it added bite. While curtido is traditionally served with pupusas, El Salvadoran tortillas stuffed with fillings, this spicy slaw can accompany a wide range of meat and vegetable dishes. If you like it hot, leave the seeds in the jalapeños.

2 green cabbage heads
   (enough to yield 1½ pounds
   cored, shredded cabbage)
3 carrots, shredded
½ onion, thinly sliced
2 jalapeños, seeded and minced
2 teaspoons sugar
1 teaspoon pickling salt
½ teaspoon red pepper flakes
¼ cup raw apple cider vinegar

1 Remove the outer leaves from the cabbage and discard. Halve and then quarter the cabbage, and cut the core from each piece. With the cut side down, slice the cabbage into thin strips between ⅛ and ¼ inch thick.

2 Combine the cabbage, carrots, onion, jalapeños, sugar, salt, and red pepper flakes in a large bowl. With clean hands, mix the ingredients, massaging the salt into the vegetables.

3 Pack the cabbage mixture into a quart jar, pressing down firmly as you go. Pour the vinegar over the kraut. Use a weight to hold the cabbage below the brine. Cover the jar with a lid and place in a cool location.

4 After 2 or 3 days, taste the curtido. If you like it, transfer it to the refrigerator to halt fermentation. If you feel it needs more time, replace the lid and continue fermenting for another 2 or 3 days, tasting daily. Transfer it to the refrigerator once it's done.

Vegetables

MAKES 1 QUART   Prep: **15 minutes** | Fermentation: **2 to 5 days** | Storage: **3 weeks**

Notes:

PREP TIP: *Most sauerkraut recipes recommend avoiding the use of a food processor, as it leaves cabbage in a near-pulverized, watery state. However, for this recipe, which has a short fermentation time, it's no problem to prep the ingredients in a food processor, if desired.*

GINGER-BEET SAUERKRAUT

Beets not only cleanse the body, they also add a subtle sweetness and loads of color to this sauerkraut. The addition of ginger gives the sauerkraut some warming tang and also enhances its digestibility. This is by far one of my favorite blends, and I can't recommend it enough. I like to make it with a mix of green and red cabbage because it looks so beautiful, but feel free to use whatever you have on hand.

2 green or red cabbage heads (enough to yield 1½ pounds cored, shredded cabbage)
1 beet, shredded
1 (2-inch) piece ginger, peeled and grated
1 clove garlic, minced
4 teaspoons pickling salt

1 Remove the outer leaves from the cabbage and discard. Halve and then quarter the cabbage, and cut the core from each piece. With the cut side down, slice the cabbage into thin strips between ⅛ and ¼ inch thick.

2 Combine the cabbage, beet, ginger, garlic, and pickling salt in a large bowl. With clean hands, mix the ingredients, massaging the salt into the cabbage. Cover the bowl with a clean kitchen towel and leave to rest at room temperature for 30 minutes.

3 Pack the vegetables into a quart jar, pressing down firmly as you go. Pour any remaining juices from the bowl into the jar. Use a weight to hold the cabbage below the brine. Cover with a lid and place in a cool location.

4 After 2 or 3 days, fermentation will have started. Check the sauerkraut every day or two, loosening the lid to "burp" out trapped gases and remove any scum that forms on the surface. Always make sure that the kraut is submerged below the brine. Re-weight the kraut, close the lid, and continue to monitor its progress. After 2 weeks, taste the kraut. At this time, it will still be crunchy and only lightly fermented. If you like it, transfer it to the refrigerator to halt fermentation. If you are not yet satisfied with the flavor, replace the lid and continue to ferment for up to 6 weeks, tasting regularly. Transfer it to the refrigerator once it's done.

Vegetables

MAKES 1 QUART

Prep: **15 minutes** | Rest: **30 minutes** | Fermentation: **2 to 6 weeks** | Storage: **6 weeks**

Notes:

PREP TIP: *To remove beet juice stains from your hands, scoop a generous amount of baking soda onto your hands, mix with a little water, and scrub vigorously. Rinse and repeat until the color fades away.*

FALL HARVEST SAUERKRAUT

Home Fermentation

If you are making sauerkraut with the seasons, come fall you may have gotten bored of the same old cabbage and salt combination. When that occurs, whip up a batch of this seasonal blend that highlights some of the best flavors of the cooler months. Fennel brings an intensely fresh, crisp seasoning and the apple lends a slight sweetness, while the leek balances the two. Slightly less sturdy than green cabbage, napa cabbage pairs well with the other crunchy components of this scrumptious kraut.

1½ pounds napa cabbage

1 small green apple, shredded

1 fennel bulb, thinly sliced

1 leek, thinly sliced

4 teaspoons pickling salt

1 Remove the outer leaves from the cabbage and discard. Halve the cabbage, and cut the core from each half. With the cut side down, slice the cabbage into thin strips between ⅛ and ¼ inch thick.

2 Combine the cabbage, apple, fennel, leek, and pickling salt in a large bowl. With clean hands, mix the ingredients, massaging the salt into the cabbage and other vegetables. Cover the bowl with a clean kitchen towel and leave to rest at room temperature for 1 hour.

3 Pack the vegetables into a quart jar, pressing down firmly as you go. Pour any juices from the bowl into the jar. Use a weight to hold the cabbage below the brine. Cover with a lid and place in a cool location.

4 After 2 or 3 days, fermentation will have started. Check the sauerkraut every day or two, loosening the lid to "burp" out trapped gases and remove any scum that forms on the surface. Make sure that the kraut is submerged below the brine. Re-weight the kraut, close the lid, and continue to monitor its progress. After 1 week, taste the kraut. It will still be crunchy and only lightly fermented. If you like it, transfer it to the refrigerator to halt fermentation. If you are not yet satisfied with the flavor, replace the lid and continue to ferment for up to 3 weeks, tasting regularly. Transfer it to the refrigerator once it's done.

MAKES 1 QUART

Prep: **15 minutes** | Rest: **1 hour** | Fermentation: **1 to 3 weeks** | Storage: **3 weeks**

Notes:

PREP TIP: *To clean the leeks, first run them under water in a colander to remove some of the exterior dirt. Then slice them and place them in a bowl. Fill the bowl with water and use your hands to agitate the leeks and remove the dirt. Change the water two or three times, until it is no longer dirty. Drain the leeks well.*

BRUSSELS SPROUT AND CABBAGE KRAUT

I love the taste of Brussels sprouts mixed with cabbage—together they blend just the right amount of bitter and sweet. For the best quality and freshest flavor, try to buy Brussels sprouts still on the stalk and cut them off yourself. As with cabbage, the fresher they are, the more natural moisture they contain—a beneficial ingredient when making a dry-salted ferment such as sauerkraut.

1 green cabbage head (enough to yield 1 pound cored, shredded cabbage)

1 pound Brussels sprouts

4 teaspoons pickling salt

1 Remove the outer leaves from the cabbage and discard. Halve and then quarter the cabbage, and cut the core from each piece. With the cut side down, slice the cabbage into thin strips between ⅛ and ¼ inch thick. Remove and discard the base of each Brussels sprout and then slice the sprouts into thin strips.

2 Combine the cabbage, Brussels sprouts, and pickling salt in a large bowl. With clean hands, mix the ingredients, massaging the salt into the cabbage. Cover the bowl with a clean kitchen towel and leave to rest at room temperature for 30 minutes.

continues ➤

Vegetables

MAKES 1 QUART

Prep: **15 minutes** | Rest: **30 minutes** | Fermentation: **2 to 6 weeks** | Storage: **6 weeks**

Notes:

MAKE IT A MEAL: *This is one of my favorite blends to pair with sausage for a simple but complete meal. To prepare, select 1 pound of your favorite type of pork or turkey sausages, and slice them into ½-inch-thick rounds. In a small pot, brown the sausage, then add about 1 quart of kraut. Cook over medium heat until both are heated through, about 10 minutes.*

BRUSSELS SPROUT AND CABBAGE KRAUT CONTINUED

3 Pack the cabbage mixture into a quart jar, pressing down firmly as you go. Pour any remaining juices from the bowl into the jar to cover the mixture. Use a weight to hold the cabbage below the brine. Cover the jar with a lid and place in a cool location.

4 After 2 or 3 days, fermentation will have started. Check the sauerkraut every day or two, loosening the lid to "burp" out any trapped gases and remove any scum that forms on the surface. Always make sure that the kraut is submerged below the brine. Re-weight the kraut, close the lid, and continue to monitor its progress. After 2 weeks, taste the kraut. At this time, it will still be quite crunchy and only lightly fermented. If you like it, transfer it to the refrigerator to halt fermentation. If you are not yet satisfied with the flavor, continue to ferment for up to 6 weeks, tasting regularly. Transfer it to the refrigerator once it's done.

SAKE-FERMENTED KRAUT

Using a brine made of sake (Japanese rice wine) and water allows you to make a salt-free sauerkraut. But because there is no added salt—the ingredient normally used to counteract spoilage—you must be extremely diligent with this kraut, so be sure to check on it daily and skim off any scum as needed, and always keep the cabbage below the brine level.

2 or 3 green cabbage heads (enough to yield 2 pounds cored, shredded cabbage)

2 cups water

½ cup sake

1 Remove the outer leaves from the cabbage and discard. Halve and then quarter the cabbage, and cut the core from each piece. With the cut side down, slice the cabbage into thin strips between ⅛ and ¼ inch thick. Pack the cabbage firmly into a quart jar, pressing it down as you go.

2 In a small bowl, mix the water and sake to create a brine, and then pour it over the cabbage. Use a weight to hold the cabbage below the brine. Cover the jar and place in a cool location.

3 After 2 or 3 days, fermentation will have started. Check the sauerkraut every day or two, loosening the lid to "burp" out any trapped gases and remove any scum that forms on the surface. Always make sure that the kraut is submerged below the brine. Re-weight the kraut, close the lid, and continue to monitor its progress. After 2 weeks, taste the kraut. At this time, it will still be quite crunchy and only lightly fermented. If you like it, transfer it to the refrigerator to halt fermentation. If you are not yet satisfied with the flavor, continue to ferment for up to 6 weeks, tasting regularly. Transfer it to the refrigerator once it's done.

Vegetables

MAKES 1 QUART   Prep: **10 minutes** | Fermentation: **2 to 6 weeks** | Storage: **6 weeks**

Notes:

CLASSIC KIMCHI

Home Fermentation

There is some debate on whether kimchi is a Korean version of sauerkraut or sauerkraut is a Westernized version of kimchi. Either way, kimchi is known for its use of napa cabbage, unlike its Western counterpart, which almost always uses green cabbage. Also called Chinese cabbage, this leafier version of cabbage is typically combined with garlic, onions, scallions, and chiles, but as with sauerkraut, the variations of kimchi are virtually endless.

3 tablespoons pickling salt, divided

4 cups water

2 pounds napa cabbage

4 garlic cloves, peeled and smashed with the back of a knife

1 small onion, thinly sliced

3 scallions, cut into 2-inch pieces

1 (1-inch) piece ginger, peeled and minced

2 tablespoons Korean ground red pepper

1 teaspoon sugar

1 In a large mixing bowl, dissolve 2½ tablespoons of the salt in the water to make a brine. Halve the cabbage and cut the leaves into 2-inch squares. Add them to the bowl with the brine. Use a plate to weight the cabbage down. Cover the bowl with a clean kitchen towel and set aside at room temperature for 8 to 12 hours.

2 Drain the cabbage, reserving the brine. In a large bowl, toss the cabbage with the garlic, onion, scallions, and ginger. Add the remaining ½ tablespoon salt, the ground red pepper, and the sugar and mix well. Pack the mixture into a quart jar and pour enough brine over the cabbage to cover. Use a weight to hold the cabbage below the brine. Close the jar with a lid and place it in a cool location (about 68°F).

3 After 3 days, taste the kimchi. If you like it, remove the weight, replace the lid, and transfer it to the refrigerator to halt fermentation. If you are not yet satisfied with the flavor, replace the lid and continue to ferment for up to 2 more days, tasting daily. Transfer it to the refrigerator once it's done.

MAKES 1 QUART

Prep: **15 minutes** | Rest: **8 to 12 hours** | Fermentation: **3 to 5 days** | Storage: **6 weeks**

Notes:

A CLOSER LOOK: *Korean chiles are a mild variety, hence their liberal use when making kimchi. Do not substitute just any hot pepper if you cannot find this product. New Mexican ground chiles are comparable when making kimchi, but can also be hard to find in some locations. If so, substitute a mixture of ground cayenne pepper and paprika in a ratio that suits your taste.*

DAIKON, CARROT, AND SCALLION KIMCHI

Regular kimchi made with mostly cabbage is great, but I really love the crunch of daikon. For this reason alone, my favorite kimchi to make is one that uses just a bit of cabbage with the bulk of the pickle rounded out by this crisp radish. Both daikon and carrots stay super crisp even through extended fermentation, and together these three vegetables burst with flavor when combined with the spice of the chiles.

2½ tablespoons pickling salt, divided

4 cups water

8 ounces napa cabbage

1 pound daikon, sliced

2 carrots, sliced

4 garlic cloves, peeled and smashed with the back of a knife

5 scallions, cut into 2-inch lengths

1 (1-inch) piece ginger, peeled and minced

2 tablespoons Korean ground red pepper

1 teaspoon sugar

1 In a large mixing bowl, dissolve 2 tablespoons of the salt in the water to make a brine. Halve the cabbage and cut the leaves into 2-inch squares. Add the cabbage, daikon, and carrots to the bowl with the brine. Use a plate to weight the vegetables down. Cover the bowl with a clean kitchen towel and set aside at room temperature for 8 to 12 hours.

2 Drain the mixture, reserving the brine. In a large bowl, toss the vegetables with the garlic, scallions, and ginger. Add the remaining ½ tablespoon salt, the ground red pepper, and the sugar and mix well. Pack the mixture into a quart jar and pour enough brine over the vegetables to cover. Use a weight to hold the cabbage below the brine. Close the jar with a lid and place it in a cool location (about 68°F).

3 After 3 days, taste the kimchi. If you like it, remove the weight, replace the lid, and transfer it to the refrigerator to halt fermentation. If the flavor is not yet to your liking, replace the lid and continue to ferment for up to 2 more days, tasting daily. Transfer it to the refrigerator once it's done.

MAKES 1 QUART

Prep: **15 minutes** | Rest: **8 to 12 hours** | Fermentation: **3 to 5 days** | Storage: **6 weeks**

- -

Notes:

- -

PREP TIP: *Daikon doesn't necessarily need to be peeled before use. Scrub off any dirty spots with a brush, and cut away blemishes if necessary, but leave the skin on to promote growth of healthy bacteria.*

MUSHROOM-KOMBU KIMCHI

Kombu, a type of seaweed, adds a distinctive flavor to this kimchi even though its only contact is in the primary soaking stage. Made with daikon, cabbage, mushrooms, and pear, this kimchi produces a sweet-spicy flavor combination bursting with character. Note that the process for this kimchi is slightly different, and leaves you with a drier, more traditional kimchi than the previous recipes.

2½ tablespoons pickling salt, divided

5 cups water, divided

1 pound napa cabbage

12 ounces daikon, sliced

1 (1-inch-by-2-inch) piece kombu

2 dried shiitake mushrooms

1 Asian pear, peeled and cored

1 (1-inch) piece ginger, peeled

1½ tablespoons Korean ground red pepper

3 scallions, cut into 2-inch pieces

1 In a large mixing bowl, dissolve 2 tablespoons of the salt in 4 cups of the water to make a brine. Halve the cabbage and cut the leaves into 2-inch squares. Add the cabbage and daikon to the bowl with the brine. Use a plate to weight the vegetables down. Cover the bowl with a clean kitchen towel and set aside at room temperature for 8 to 12 hours.

2 In a small bowl, combine the remaining 1 cup water, the kombu, and the mushrooms and set aside at room temperature for 30 minutes. Remove the mushrooms and slice them very thin. Discard the water and kombu.

3 Drain the cabbage, squeezing it to remove any excess liquid, and return it to the bowl; discard the brine. Combine the pear and ginger in a food processor and process until it forms a paste. Add the ground red pepper and the remaining ½ tablespoon salt and mix well. Transfer the paste to the bowl with the cabbage and, using your hands, massage it thoroughly into the cabbage. Mix in the scallion segments. Pack the mixture into a quart jar, leaving about 1 inch of headspace. Use a weight to hold the cabbage down. At this point, the cabbage will not be submerged, but within a day, a brine will form. Close the jar with a lid and place in a cool location (about 68°F).

continues ▶

MAKES 1 QUART

Prep: **15 minutes** | Rest: **8 to 12 hours** | Fermentation: **3 to 6 days** | Storage: **6 weeks**

Notes:

A CLOSER LOOK: *Kombu is a natural flavor enhancer, and in 1940s Japan, monosodium glutamate (MSG) was extracted from kombu's naturally occurring glutamic acid for use in flavoring foods. While the synthetic variety of MSG is harmful to the body, this naturally occurring flavor enhancer is actually good for you.*

4 After 3 days, taste the kimchi. If you like it, remove the weight, replace the lid, and transfer it to the refrigerator to halt fermentation. If you're not yet satisfied with the taste, replace the lid and continue to ferment for up to 3 more days, tasting daily. Transfer it to the refrigerator once it's done.

DAIKON KIMCHI

This fiery kimchi is all bite and no nonsense. Fish sauce adds a distinctive element to this simple mixture that sets it apart from the rest. Try tasting it after just 1 day and see what you think—I love it after either a single day or the full 3 days, as the flavors are different, yet both are so delicious. Serve this kimchi with just about any Asian-style meal.

1½ pounds daikon, peeled and cut into 1-inch cubes

1½ teaspoons pickling salt

1 teaspoon sugar

4 garlic cloves, peeled and minced

3 scallions, cut into 2-inch pieces

1 (1-inch) piece ginger, peeled and minced

1 tablespoon fish sauce

2 tablespoons Korean ground red pepper

1 In a large mixing bowl, toss the daikon cubes with the salt and sugar. Cover the bowl with a clean kitchen towel and set aside for 30 minutes. Drain the daikon, reserving the juices in a small bowl.

2 Add the garlic, scallions, ginger, fish sauce, and ground red pepper to the daikon and toss. Pack the mixture into a quart jar, pressing down as you go to remove air bubbles. Add the reserved daikon juices. Use a weight to hold the daikon below the brine. Affix a lid and leave the kimchi to ferment at room temperature for up to 3 days. Transfer to the refrigerator to halt fermentation.

MAKES 1 QUART

Prep: **15 minutes** | Rest: **30 minutes** | Fermentation: **1 to 3 days** | Storage: **3 weeks**

Notes:

PREP TIP: *I prefer to cut the daikon into cubes for this single-vegetable ferment. They are fun to eat in cubes, but the larger chunks also make this spicy ferment more palatable, as there is more surface area of actual radish instead of just hot pepper. If you prefer a different cut, go for it, but keep in mind that you will be adding a significant amount of hot pepper to the batch.*

CUCUMBER KIMCHI

Cucumber kimchi is not meant to be stored for as long as other types of kimchi—it should be eaten in just a few days. Cucumbers lose their crunch, and the crunch is part of their appeal. However, I never have a problem going through a jar of this, as I never tire of its complex, tantalizing flavor.

1 pound pickling cucumbers, cut into 1- to 2-inch chunks

1½ teaspoons pickling salt

2 garlic cloves, peeled and smashed with the back of a knife

2 scallions, cut on the bias into 1-inch pieces

2 tablespoons finely chopped onion

½ teaspoon white vinegar

½ teaspoon raw honey

1 tablespoon Korean ground red pepper

1 In a large mixing bowl, toss the cucumbers and salt. Cover the bowl with a clean kitchen towel and set aside at room temperature for 8 to 12 hours.

2 Add the garlic, scallions, onion, vinegar, honey, and red pepper and toss well. Pack the mixture into a pint jar, lightly pressing the cucumbers down as you go. Pour any liquid left in the bowl over the vegetables. Affix a lid and leave at room temperature for up to 2 days. Transfer to the refrigerator to halt fermentation.

MAKES 1 PINT

Prep: **10 minutes** | Rest: **8 to 12 hours** | Fermentation: **1 to 2 days** | Storage: **5 days**

Notes:

TURMERIC-GARLIC DILL PICKLES

Get a little nutrient boost with these tasty pickles that combine the anti-inflammatory protection of turmeric with the digestive-boosting qualities of garlic. Whether served as a quick snack or alongside a meal, these pickles make a great addition to your usual routine, not only for their health benefits, but because they taste great, too. The finished pickles are tinged with turmeric's distinctive yellow color, giving them a character that sets them apart.

2 grape leaves (optional)

1 dill head, including dill fronds

10 garlic cloves, peeled and
   smashed with the back of a knife

5 black peppercorns

1½ teaspoons ground turmeric

1¼ pounds pickling cucumbers,
   blossom ends trimmed

1¾ tablespoons pickling salt

2½ cups water

1 In a quart jar, combine the grape leaves (if using), dill, garlic, peppercorns, and turmeric. Pack the cucumbers tightly into the jar.

2 In a small bowl, dissolve the salt in the water, and pour this brine over the cucumbers. If necessary, use a weight to hold the cucumbers down. Cover the jar with a clean kitchen towel and set aside at room temperature.

3 After 2 or 3 days, fermentation will have started, and bubbles will begin rising to the surface. Check the pickles daily, removing any scum that forms on the surface and making sure that the cucumbers remain submerged below the brine.

4 When the bubbles stop rising, fermentation is complete; however, you may begin tasting the pickles after about a week. When they taste good to you, cap the jar with a nonreactive lid and transfer to the refrigerator to halt fermentation.

MAKES 1 QUART   Prep: **10 minutes** | Fermentation: **1 to 4 weeks** | Storage: **1 to 2 months**

Notes:

PREP TIP: *If desired, you can also make halves or spears with these pickles instead of leaving them whole. To do this, before fermentation, simply slice the cucumbers lengthwise in half and then into quarters, depending on the size. This may allow you to fit slightly more cucumbers in the jar.*

BREAD AND BUTTER SLICES

If you like a sweet pickle on your burgers, this is the recipe for you. These lovely little slices are super quick and easy to throw together, and you can enjoy them for months to come. The soaking step keeps the cucumbers fresh, providing that desirable snap when you bite into a sandwich loaded with these sweet slices.

3 cups sliced pickling cucumbers

1 small onion, sliced

1 dried red chile, slit lengthwise

¼ cup freshly squeezed lemon juice

¼ cup raw honey

2 tablespoons whey (page 31)

1 tablespoon pickling salt

2 teaspoons celery seeds

1 teaspoon mustard seeds

1 Soak the cucumber slices in a bowl of ice water placed in the refrigerator for at least 2 hours and as long as 6 hours before beginning the fermenting process.

2 Drain the cucumbers. Mix the cucumber slices, onion slices, and chile in a large bowl, then pack them into a quart jar, pressing down as you go.

3 In a small bowl, mix the lemon juice, honey, whey, salt, celery seeds, and mustard seeds and pour this mixture over the cucumbers. Fill the remaining space in the jar with water, leaving 1 inch of headspace. If needed, weight the cucumbers with a small weight to keep them submerged. Cap the jar loosely and let the pickles ferment at room temperature for 2 or 3 days. Transfer the jar to the refrigerator to halt fermentation.

MAKES 1 QUART

Prep: **10 minutes** | Rest: **2 to 6 hours** | Fermentation: **2 to 3 days** | Storage: **2 to 3 months**

Notes:

LACTO-FERMENTED ICICLE PICKLES

If you like sweet spears, these are a great alternative to the vinegar-pickled variety. Requiring just a couple of days for fermentation, these are promptly ready to go, allowing you to savor their sweet and slightly sour flavor even sooner than the so-called quick-pickled varieties that actually call for several weeks of curing. I think these offer a pleasing dose of sweetness without being cloying, but feel free to play around with the level of maple syrup added to suit your taste, especially if you are watching your sugar intake.

1 pound pickling cucumbers, blossom ends trimmed

½ cup pure maple syrup

3 whole cloves

1 teaspoon mustard seeds

½ teaspoon whole allspice berries

⅛ teaspoon red pepper flakes

2 tablespoons freshly squeezed lemon juice

2 tablespoons whey (page 31)

2 teaspoons pickling salt

1 small onion, thinly sliced

1 Cut the cucumbers into spears and soak them in a bowl of ice water for 1 hour.

2 Meanwhile, in a small saucepan over medium-high heat, bring the maple syrup, cloves, mustard seeds, allspice, and red pepper flakes to a boil. As soon as the mixture comes to a boil, remove the pan from the heat. Cool the mixture to room temperature, then stir in the lemon juice, whey, and salt.

3 Drain the cucumbers. Pack the spears into a quart jar, layering with the onion slices. Pour the cooled brine over the cucumbers. Fill the remaining space in the jar with water, leaving 1 inch of headspace.

4 If needed, weight the cucumbers with a small weight to keep them submerged in the brine. Affix a lid and let the pickles ferment at room temperature for 2 days. Transfer to the refrigerator and chill for 2 to 3 days before eating.

MAKES 1 QUART   Prep: **15 minutes** | Rest: **1 hour** | Fermentation: **2 days** | Storage: **1 month**

Notes:

FERMENTED CURRIED ZUCCHINI

Zucchini are prolific growers. One moment you have a couple of zucchini, and then seemingly overnight you can be overwhelmed by the production of just one plant. I love fermenting the small ones, which end up tasting quite a bit like cucumber pickles. Try to pick zucchini under 6 inches long so they don't contain any hardened seeds. If you have a substantial crop and some have grown especially large, however, they can still be used. Simply cut them in half, scoop out the seeds, and slice the remaining flesh as usual.

4 cups sliced zucchini

5 garlic cloves, peeled and smashed with the back of a knife

2 tablespoons curry powder

1½ teaspoons pickling salt

2 cups water

1 Pack the zucchini and garlic into a quart jar. In a small bowl, mix the curry powder and salt into the water and stir to dissolve the salt. Pour this brine over the zucchini. Weight the zucchini down below the brine. Cap the jar and let ferment at room temperature.

2 After about 2 days, you will see bubbles rising, signaling the start of fermentation. Check the zucchini every day or two, loosening the lid to "burp" out any trapped gases and remove any scum that forms on the surface. Always make sure that the zucchini are submerged below the brine. Fermentation is complete when the bubbles stop rising to the surface, 5 to 7 days. Replace the cap and transfer to the refrigerator to halt fermentation.

MAKES 1 QUART   Prep: **10 minutes** | Fermentation: **5 to 7 days** | Storage: **2 to 3 months**

Notes:

MAKE IT A MEAL: *I serve this type of ferment as a side dish with a simple meal such as baked chicken and rice. The flavors in the curry powder play well off other lightly seasoned foods, and pair nicely with sides like rice, roasted potatoes, or other roasted root vegetables.*

FERMENTED CAULIFLOWER

Thankfully, the crispness of cauliflower is not lost during the fermentation process. While many vegetables will become softer, cauliflower holds its own against the test of the pickling liquid. Choose a small cauliflower head, or break off what you need to fill a jar. Either way, make sure you pack the cauliflower firmly in the jar to get in as much as possible— you will be glad you made the extra effort when this pickle is complete.

1 small cauliflower head,
   separated into small florets
3 garlic cloves, peeled and
   smashed with the back of a knife
1 dried chile, slit lengthwise
1 tablespoon pickling salt

1 Pack the cauliflower, garlic, and chile into a quart jar and add the salt. Fill the jar with water, leaving 1 inch of headspace. Apply the lid and give the jar a good shake to mix the salt with the water. Open the jar, weight the cauliflower down below the brine, and replace the cap. Let it ferment at room temperature.

2 After about 2 days, you will see bubbles rising, signaling the start of fermentation. Check the cauliflower every day or two, loosening the lid to "burp" out any trapped gases and remove any scum that forms on the surface. Always make sure that the cauliflower is submerged below the brine. Fermentation is complete when the bubbles stop rising to the surface, 5 to 7 days. Tighten the lid and transfer to the refrigerator to halt fermentation.

MAKES 1 QUART   Prep: **10 minutes** | Fermentation: **5 to 7 days** | Storage: **2 to 3 months**

Notes:

A CLOSER LOOK: *Cauliflower is a member of the brassica family of plants, which also includes broccoli and cabbage. Like other brassica members, it contains antioxidant, antibiotic, anticancer, and antiviral properties. It is quite similar in nutritional value to broccoli but contains a lower amount of many vitamins and minerals than its green cousin.*

FERMENTED BROCCOLI AND CAULIFLOWER

The green and white colors of this ferment look great together, and the flavors are pretty well matched, too. The ginger and coriander are both highly evident in this crunchy brassica family medley. While broccoli and cauliflower are most often eaten cooked, they have the highest vitamin and mineral content when in their raw state. Pickling makes them more digestible (and delicious), so if you don't like eating either of these vegetables raw, you may want to give them another chance with this ferment.

1½ cups cauliflower florets

1½ cups broccoli florets

2 scallions, thinly sliced

1 apple, cored and diced

½ teaspoon coriander seeds

1 (1-inch) piece ginger, peeled and grated

2 tablespoons pickling salt

2 cups water

1 In a large bowl, toss the cauliflower, broccoli, scallions, apple, coriander seeds, and ginger. Pack the mixture into a quart jar, pressing down firmly as you go. In a small bowl, dissolve the salt in the water, and pour this brine over the vegetables. Weight the vegetables down and affix a lid to the jar. Let the vegetables ferment at room temperature.

2 After about 2 days, you will see bubbles rising, signaling the start of fermentation. Check the vegetables every day or two, loosening the lid to "burp" out any trapped gases and remove any scum that forms on the surface. Always make sure that the vegetables are submerged below the brine. Fermentation is complete when the bubbles stop rising to the surface, 5 to 7 days. Replace the cap and transfer to the refrigerator to halt fermentation.

MAKES 1 QUART   Prep: **10 minutes** | Fermentation: **5 to 7 days** | Storage: **2 to 3 months**

Notes:

FERMENTED CELERY

Celery is especially good when fresh from the farm toward the end of summer. This crisp, sweet crop is the best for fermenting—and, of course, for eating raw. If you can't get it direct from the farm, any store-bought variety will work, but be sure to include plenty of the tender inner ribs, which are sweeter than the outer ones. A close relative of parsley, the celery plant is 100 percent edible, from the stalks to the leaves and seeds. If the leaves look good, add some to the ferment and see what you think.

1 small bunch celery, cut into
    1-inch pieces
5 garlic cloves, peeled and
    smashed with the back of a knife
½ onion, sliced
1 dill head
1 tablespoon pickling salt
4 cups water

1 Pack the celery, garlic, onion, and dill into a quart jar, layering as you go. In a small bowl, dissolve the salt in the water, and pour this brine over the vegetables. Weight the celery down, and close the jar. Let it ferment at room temperature.

2 After about 2 days, you will see bubbles rising, signaling the start of fermentation. Check the celery every day or two, loosening the lid to "burp" out any trapped gases and remove any scum that forms on the surface. Always make sure that the celery is submerged below the brine. Fermentation is complete when the bubbles stop rising to the surface, 5 to 7 days. Replace the cap and transfer to the refrigerator to halt fermentation.

MAKES 1 QUART   Prep: **10 minutes** | Fermentation: **5 to 7 days** | Storage: **2 to 3 months**

Notes:

A CLOSER LOOK: *When selecting celery at the store, look for firm bunches that have green, crisp leaves. Keep in mind that celery is a heavily sprayed crop, which is typically treated with ethylene gas after picking to minimize its bitter flavor. For these reasons, choosing organic celery is advisable.*

FERMENTED RADISHES

Fermented radishes are at the top of my all-time favorite ferments list. As soon as fresh radishes are available in late spring, I begin making this ferment and continue to replenish my supplies well through the fall. While you can enhance the flavor with mustard seeds, coriander seeds, garlic, bay leaves, and other aromatics, I prefer the simplicity of the plain radish ferment. I use these on green salads, pasta salads, and grain salads, and I have also been known to eat them straight from the jar.

4 bunches radishes, sliced
1 tablespoon pickling salt
2 cups water

1 Pack the radish slices into a quart jar. In a small bowl, dissolve the salt in the water, and pour this brine over the radishes.

2 Weight the radishes to keep them submerged in the brine and affix a lid to the jar. Let the radishes ferment at room temperature.

3 After about 2 days, you will see bubbles rising, signaling the start of fermentation. Check the radishes every day or two, loosening the lid to "burp" out any trapped gases and remove any scum that forms on the surface. Always make sure that the radishes are submerged below the brine. Fermentation is complete when bubbles stop rising to the surface. However, you can begin tasting the radishes after about 5 days. When they are adequately soured, transfer them to the refrigerator to halt fermentation.

MAKES 1 QUART   Prep: **10 minutes** | Fermentation: **5 to 7 days** | Storage: **1 to 2 months**

Notes:

PREP TIP: *I enjoy using a range of varieties when making a quart of fermented radishes. Try using a mixture of French radishes, Easter egg radishes, and red globe radishes when you make this recipe. Each radish has its own different texture and flavor, and even though they taste similar, once they are fermented, differences in texture remain.*

FERMENTED DAIKON

Daikon maintains an amazing crunch even after fermentation, making this formidable radish one of the best fermenters around. Silky white in color, daikon can grow to be several feet long, but is often cut into more reasonable lengths for sale in supermarkets. If you like daikon, buy a large one and double this recipe, or use the remaining portion for another recipe in this book—don't be afraid to have extra, as it keeps well in the refrigerator, stored in a plastic bag in the crisper drawer. Serve the finished ferment alongside an Asian-style meal that will make it shine.

1 pound daikon, cut into
   matchsticks

1 (2-inch) piece ginger,
   peeled and sliced

4 garlic cloves, peeled and
   smashed with the back of a knife

3 small dried chiles

1½ tablespoons pickling salt

2 cups water

1 Pack the daikon sticks into a quart jar, alternating with the ginger, garlic, and chiles. In a small bowl, dissolve the salt in the water, and pour this brine over the daikon. Use a weight to submerge the daikon below the brine. Close the jar and let the daikon ferment at room temperature.

2 Start tasting the daikon after 3 days; when it is soured to your liking, replace the cap and transfer to the refrigerator to halt fermentation.

MAKES 1 QUART Prep: **10 minutes** | Fermentation: **3 to 6 days** | Storage: **1 month**

Notes:

FERMENTED GREEN BEANS

If you enjoy vinegar-pickled green beans, you will simply love these. Prepared using just salt, water, and spices, this simple ferment is super easy to make at home, and when it comes to cost, there's no comparison to the high prices you'd pay for a similar product at the market. Customize this recipe to your own palate, and enjoy these beans with all the snap of a pickle in salads, stir-fries, or, my favorite, a Bloody Mary.

12 ounces young green beans, trimmed

2 dill heads or 1 tablespoon dried dill

4 to 6 garlic cloves, peeled and smashed with the back of a knife

8 black peppercorns, crushed

2 tablespoons pickling salt

3 cups water

1 Pack the beans into a quart jar, layering with the dill, garlic, and peppercorns. In a small bowl, dissolve the salt in the water, and pour this brine over the beans. Weight the beans, if necessary, to keep them submerged in the brine, and affix a lid to the jar. Let ferment at room temperature.

2 After about 2 days, you will see bubbles rising, signaling the start of fermentation. Check the beans every day or two, loosening the lid to "burp" out any trapped gases and remove any scum that forms on the surface. Always make sure that the beans are submerged below the brine. Fermentation is complete when bubbles stop rising to the surface. Begin checking the beans for doneness at about 2 weeks. When they've soured to your liking, replace the lid and transfer them to the refrigerator to halt fermentation.

Vegetables

MAKES 1 QUART   Prep: **20 minutes** | Fermentation: **2 to 3 weeks** | Storage: **1 to 2 months**

Notes:

A CLOSER LOOK: *Any good-tasting green bean can be used to make pickled beans. The most common varieties grown for pickling tend to be Blue Lake and Kentucky beans, but that doesn't mean you are limited to these. Experiment with other beans from your garden or market—just make sure that they are young and tender.*

FERMENTED CARROTS

Carrots are nutrient dense and a perfect food for on-the-go snacking, but because they lack significant flavor on their own, they are often underutilized in the kitchen. However, the story is completely different with fermented carrots. Teeming with flavor, these sticks will fly out of the jar faster than you can make them. For kids, these are especially fun to make, and they love eating them, too. Pair them with Creamy Kefir Salad Dressing (page 179), and you will be struggling to keep up with your household's demand for this healthy snack.

5 garlic cloves, peeled and smashed with the back of a knife

1 teaspoon pickling spice

1 pound carrots, washed and cut into sticks

1¾ teaspoons pickling salt

2½ cups water

1 Combine the garlic and pickling spice in a quart jar. Add the carrots, packing them in tightly. In a small bowl, dissolve the salt in the water, and pour this brine over the carrots. If necessary, weight the carrots down to keep them submerged in the brine. Cap the jar and let the carrots ferment at room temperature.

2 After about 2 days, you will see bubbles rising, signaling the start of fermentation. Check the carrots every day or two, loosening the lid to "burp" out any trapped gases and remove any scum that forms on the surface. Always make sure that the carrots are submerged below the brine. Fermentation is complete when the bubbles stop rising to the surface, 5 to 7 days. At this time, replace the cap and transfer to the refrigerator to halt fermentation.

MAKES 1 QUART   Prep: **10 minutes** | Fermentation: **5 to 7 days** | Storage: **2 to 3 months**

- -

Notes:

- -

PREP TIP: If you don't like the idea of carrot sticks, grate the carrots instead to make a different type of ferment. Using the same seasonings, I ferment this mixture for 3 to 5 days; when finished, I use it in simple green salads for extra flavor. Add some nuts and dried fruit, and you have a quick and filling meal.

SPICY FERMENTED GREEN BEANS

Bloody Marys are one of my favorite adult beverages, and part of the reason is that I love all the pickles that can be stuffed into the glass. I load up on nontraditional pickles like these, which are nice and spicy and add some zip to a refreshing summertime drink. Whether you use these to garnish a drink or eat them straight from the jar, you should definitely try your hand at this grown-up spicy cousin of the dilly bean.

12 ounces young green beans, trimmed

6 garlic cloves, peeled and smashed with the back of a knife

2 or 3 Thai chiles, slit lengthwise

8 black peppercorns

¼ to ½ teaspoon red pepper flakes

2 tablespoons pickling salt

3 cups water

1 Pack the beans into a quart jar, layering with the garlic, chiles, peppercorns, and red pepper flakes. In a small bowl, dissolve the salt in the water, and pour this brine over the beans. Weight the beans, if necessary, to keep them submerged in the brine, and affix a lid to the jar. Let ferment at room temperature.

2 After about 2 days, you will see bubbles rising, signaling the start of fermentation. Check the beans every day or two, loosening the lid to "burp" out any trapped gases and remove any scum that forms on the surface. Always make sure that the beans are submerged below the brine. Fermentation is complete when bubbles stop rising to the surface and the beans change color slightly. Begin tasting the beans after 1 week. When they are pickled to your liking, transfer them to the refrigerator to halt fermentation.

MAKES 1 QUART   Prep: **20 minutes** | Fermentation: **8 to 12 days** | Storage: **1 to 2 months**

Notes:

FERMENTED GARLIC SCAPES

Scapes are the flower stalk of hard-neck garlic plants, and are typically harvested in late spring. The window to buy fresh garlic scapes is quite slim, but if you manage to find some, I suggest you pickle them. Not only will you be able to savor them a bit longer, but you will also be treated to the fantastic crunch of this surprising pickle. Because the scape possesses so much character on its own, I prefer this simple ferment using just water and salt. If you want to add the "flowers" of the garlic as well, ensure that they are tightly sealed before using, as they can lead to spoilage when opened.

1½ pounds garlic scapes
1½ tablespoons pickling salt
3 cups water

1 Trim the garlic scapes to fit in a quart jar, and pack them into the jar. In a small bowl, dissolve the salt in the water, and pour this brine over the scapes. Weight down the scapes using a small weight, and affix a lid. Let ferment at room temperature.

2 After about 2 days, you will see bubbles rising, signaling the start of fermentation. Check the scapes every day or two, loosening the lid to "burp" out any trapped gases and remove any scum that forms on the surface. Always make sure that the scapes are submerged below the brine. Fermentation is complete when bubbles stop rising to the surface, but you can begin tasting the scapes after 1 week. When the scapes are pickled to your liking, transfer them to the refrigerator to halt fermentation.

MAKES 1 QUART   Prep: **10 minutes** | Fermentation: **1 to 3 weeks** | Storage: **1 to 2 months**

Notes:

FERMENTED GARLIC

Fermenting is a great way to preserve a large garlic supply. I make fermented garlic once a year in the early summer when my overwintering garlic is harvested. When using fresh garlic, less peeling is required, as garlic skins are tender and edible. If you're purchasing garlic rather than using homegrown, you can skip the step of peeling by purchasing bags of already-peeled garlic cloves in the refrigerated produce section at your grocery store.

**6 to 8 garlic heads, cloves
   separated and peeled**
1 tablespoon pickling salt
2 cups water

1   Pack the garlic cloves into a quart jar. In a small bowl, dissolve the salt in the water, and pour this brine over the garlic cloves. Weight the garlic cloves to keep them submerged in the brine, and affix a lid to the jar. Let ferment at room temperature.

2   After about 2 days, you will see bubbles rising, signaling the start of fermentation. Check the garlic every day or two, loosening the lid to "burp" out any trapped gases and remove any scum that forms on the surface. Always make sure that the garlic is submerged below the brine. Re-weight the garlic, close the lid, and continue to monitor its progress. Fermentation is complete when bubbles stop rising to the surface and the garlic develops a slightly translucent appearance. At this point, transfer the jar to the refrigerator to halt fermentation.

MAKES 1 QUART   Prep: **20 minutes** | Fermentation: **8 to 12 days** | Storage: **6 to 12 months**

Notes:

PREP TIP: *To quickly peel garlic cloves, put all the cloves in a large bowl. Place another bowl of the same size upside-down on top of this bowl. Hold the openings of the bowls together and shake the garlic-filled bowls as hard as you can until all of the skins are removed.*

LACTO-FERMENTED ASPARAGUS

Asparagus is a voracious grower once spring has officially arrived. If you are struggling to keep up with your garden, or simply want to savor the taste a little longer than its short growing window, fermenting a batch of asparagus is a great way to go. Maintaining a nice, crisp texture is easy, and the taste of this transformation is a must-try. For added color in the jar, use a mixture of white and green varieties.

1 tablespoon mustard seeds

4 garlic cloves, peeled and
  smashed with the back of a knife

1 pound asparagus,
  woody ends removed

1 tablespoon pickling salt

2 cups water

1 Combine the mustard seeds and garlic cloves in a quart jar. Pack the asparagus into the jar. In a small bowl, dissolve the salt in the water, and pour this brine over the asparagus. Gently weight the asparagus, if necessary, to keep it submerged in the brine, and affix a lid to the jar. Let ferment at room temperature.

2 After about 2 days, you will see bubbles rising, signaling the start of fermentation. Check the asparagus every day or two, loosening the lid to "burp" out any trapped gases and remove any scum that forms on the surface. Always make sure that the asparagus is submerged below the brine. Re-weight the asparagus, close the lid, and continue to monitor its progress. Fermentation is complete when bubbles stop rising to the surface. Begin tasting the asparagus at 1 week. When it is pickled to your liking, transfer the jar to the refrigerator to halt fermentation.

Vegetables

MAKES 1 QUART Prep: **20 minutes** | Fermentation: **1 to 2 weeks** | Storage: **1 to 2 months**

Notes:

PREP TIP: *To remove the woody ends of asparagus spears without using a knife, grab the spear by the base and, about midway up, bend it until it snaps. This simple trick is effective in removing the tough part of the spear, as it will naturally break where the tender part begins.*

FERMENTED MUSTARD GREENS

In Chinese cooking, fermented mustard greens make a regular appearance, yet in Western fermenting circles, they never managed to catch on as other vegetables did. However, they are deliciously spicy and complex and make a great addition to soups and stir-fries. If you pick mustard greens from your garden, aim for early spring or fall greens, which are less bitter than those produced in the heat of the summer.

8 ounces mustard greens, cut into 2-inch chunks

2 whole star anise

2 dried chiles

1 teaspoon Sichuan peppercorns

1 (1-inch) piece ginger, peeled and thinly sliced

3 tablespoons pickling salt

1 teaspoon sugar

3 cups water

1 Pack the mustard greens tightly into a quart jar; they should fill up only about three-quarters of the jar. Add the star anise, chiles, peppercorns, and ginger. In a small bowl, dissolve the salt and sugar in the water, and pour this brine over the greens. Weight the greens down to keep them submerged in the brine, and affix a lid to the jar. Let ferment at room temperature.

2 After about 2 days, you will see bubbles rising, signaling the start of fermentation. Check the greens every day or two, loosening the lid to "burp" out any trapped gases and remove any scum that forms on the surface. Always make sure that the greens are submerged below the brine. Re-weight the greens, close the lid, and continue to monitor its progress. Fermentation is complete when bubbles stop rising to the surface and the greens darken in appearance. Begin tasting the greens after 1 week. When they are pickled to your liking, affix the lid and transfer to the refrigerator to halt fermentation.

MAKES 1 QUART   Prep: **20 minutes** | Fermentation: **1 to 3 weeks** | Storage: **6 to 12 months**

Notes:

A CLOSER LOOK: *Several types of mustard greens are available at most markets. Two of the most common are curled mustard greens and purple mustard greens. I prefer to use the purple mustard greens for this ferment, as they are quite tender and have a milder flavor than the curled variety.*

GINGERED LACTO-FERMENTED BEETS

There is no shortage of methods to prepare fermented beets. This is by far one of my favorites, which long ago surpassed my previous favorite canned version. Unlike that recipe, these contain no added sugar, making them even better for your health. Add in the probiotic benefit, and these are just about the best snack around. I think they taste best after about 1 month in the refrigerator, but feel free to eat them before if you can't wait that long. Serve these beets sliced on a salad for a filling meal.

1½ pounds beets

1 cinnamon stick

1 (2-inch) piece ginger,
   peeled and sliced

3 whole cloves

2 tablespoons pickling salt

2 cups water

1 Cut off the roots and tops of the beets, and cut them into 1½-inch-long matchsticks. Pack the beets into a quart jar, along with the cinnamon, ginger, and cloves. In a small bowl, dissolve the salt in the water, and pour this brine over the beets.

2 Weight the beets down if needed, and close the jar. Let ferment at room temperature for 5 days, loosening the lid every day or two to "burp" out any trapped gases and remove any scum that forms on the surface. Transfer the beets to the refrigerator to halt fermentation, and let them cure for an additional month before eating.

MAKES 1 QUART

Prep: **10 minutes** | Fermentation: **5 days, plus 1 month curing** | Storage: **2 to 3 months**

Notes:

PREP TIP: *When fermenting beets, the skin is typically left on. This is because the skin is where the healthy microorganisms that take over the ferment are found. To get the skin really clean (because who wants dirt in their pickles?), use a produce brush and scrub the beets well under cold running water.*

CHAPTER FIVE

Fruits

- -

The first fruit ferments may very well have been alcoholic ones
such as wine, but we have come a long way since then. Today, fruit
ferments, much like vegetable ones, can be simple blends that allow
you to get more probiotics into your body on a daily basis. The dawn
of refrigeration gave us the ability to start and then stop fermentation,
producing sweet and slightly soured fruit masterpieces unlike any
other type of fermented food. In this chapter, you will learn how to
preserve your favorite fruits at their peak, and transform them into
complex and wonderfully unique probiotic powerhouses.

Recipes

FRUIT FERMENTATION BASICS

It takes much less time to ferment fruit than it does to ferment vegetables, and fruit fermentation comes with its own set of rules and guidelines.

Getting Prepared

• **Keep prep on target with recipes.** Fruit ferments are typically done within a day or two. For this reason, it is important that you not change the preparation method listed in these recipes, as it can affect whether or not fermentation is successful.

• **Swap like fruits, but don't go far off course.** You are more than welcome to switch fruits, but be sure to keep them in the same categories as those listed. Exchange berries for other berries, stone fruits for other stone fruits, and so on.

• **Keep ratios in mind.** You can adjust seasonings, but salt, whey, and other starter cultures are key to successful fermentation. Make sure you keep these in the same proportions to fruit as specified in the recipes.

The Fermentation Process

• **Apply gentle pressure.** When you are packing fruits into the jar, be careful to prevent bruising and damaging them. For fruits that are left whole, use only a gentle palm to press fruits down.

• **Submerge the fruit.** Most fruits will be submerged in a brine throughout fermentation and should be kept below this brine for the entire process. The exceptions to this rule are jams and syrups, which are entirely nonsolid. In these cases, just ensure that there are no dried fruit pieces on the walls of the jars, which are prone to becoming moldy. Use a clean paper towel to wipe down the inner surface of the jar if needed.

• **Don't wait for visual changes.** Fruit ferments require a short fermentation time to prevent them from becoming alcoholic. For this reason, adhere to the fermentation times suggested in each recipe.

• **Release gases.** It is important that you "burp" the jar every couple of days to allow built-up gases to escape. Do this by loosening the lid until you hear the gases release, and then tighten it up again.

Fruits

FRUIT
TROUBLESHOOTING TIPS

Not fermenting. With most of the ferments in this chapter, you will not see noticeable signs of fermentation. This is normal and does not mean there is a problem. After just 2 days at room temperature, there will be little, if any, movement in your fruit ferments. However, in this time, the flavor will change slightly, and this should be noticeable to you. Transfer the ferment to the refrigerator and, when chilled, try it and see what you think.

Foul smell. Pickled fruits will not smell as strongly as vegetables such as sauerkraut, and they should certainly not smell foul or putrid. If they do, toss them.

Mold on top. If mold begins to grow on the surface of the fruits, there is a problem. Again, this is not typical, but it can occur when fruits are old before they are fermented, or when they are fermented at higher than usual temperatures. Your best defense against mold is to make sure that the fruits are fresh and fully submerged during fermentation, and that you are fermenting in a cool environment that does not rise above 72°F. Also, be sure that there are no fruit scraps or residue on the interior sides of the jars. For the best results, use a clean paper towel to wipe these off before sealing the jar.

Smells like alcohol. Occasionally, when fruits are allowed to ferment for too long or in an environment that is too warm, they can become alcoholic. If this occurs, the ferment should be discarded. In the future, try transferring to cold storage sooner or fermenting in a cooler location.

Slimy texture. A slimy texture in fermentation always indicates spoilage. Do not taste this ferment; simply throw it out and try again. Pay close attention to ratios of salt, whey, and other starter cultures in subsequent recipes, and try moving your ferments to a cooler location where this is less likely to occur.

starter recipe FERMENTED LEMONS

MAKES 1 QUART   Prep: **10 minutes** | Fermentation: **1 month** | Storage: **6 months**

Preserved lemons are a distinctive ingredient of world food culture, finding their way to far-flung plates in Italy, Morocco, and India. As with many other ferments, lemons were brined and fermented as a way to preserve the harvest and add a uniquely piquant flavoring to a variety of dishes ranging from main courses to desserts. Be sure to source organic lemons when possible, as you will be using the entire fruit. Use standard, thick-skinned lemons, not Meyer lemons, for this project.

14 organic lemons
¾ cup pickling salt

1   Halve 7 of the lemons and juice them into a bowl.

2   Cut the remaining 7 lemons into slices about ½ inch thick. Pack the lemon slices into a quart jar, layering about 1½ teaspoons of salt between each slice. Press the slices down gently as you pack the jar, extracting some of the juices.

continues ►

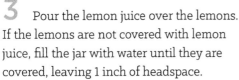

3   Pour the lemon juice over the lemons. If the lemons are not covered with lemon juice, fill the jar with water until they are covered, leaving 1 inch of headspace.

4   Affix a lid loosely, and leave the jar at room temperature for 1 month, then transfer to the refrigerator to halt fermentation.

Home Fermentation

Notes:

A CLOSER LOOK: *One of the most common uses for fermented lemons is in Moroccan tagines. Akin to a rich stew, this traditional meal is cooked over a hot charcoal fire in a covered earthenware dish (called a tagine). Consisting of meats, vegetables, poultry, or fish, these hearty stews are punctuated by the flavor of sweet and sour lemon pickles.*

LACTO-FERMENTED BERRIES

Fermenting berries may seem like an odd practice, but let me tell you—it's delicious! Giving the berries an added layer of complexity, this simple step also increases their nutritional value and gives them a pleasing sweet-sour flavor. Serve fermented berries over oatmeal or cereal or on a salad, or use them to make smoothies. For an even sweeter dish, serve them over ice cream or frozen yogurt. To infuse additional flavor into the berries, try adding a sprig of mint, basil, or rosemary to the ferment.

2 cups blackberries, blueberries, raspberries, or boysenberries

1 (1-inch) piece ginger, peeled and sliced

2 tablespoons raw honey

2 tablespoons whey (page 31)

¼ teaspoon pickling salt

1 Place the berries in a pint jar and lightly press them down with a clean spoon. Pack the ginger slices into the jar. In a small bowl, combine the honey, whey, and salt, and pour this mixture over the berries. Apply a light weight to hold the berries down, and add water to the jar until it just covers the berries.

2 Affix a lid to the jar and leave it at room temperature for 12 to 24 hours. Transfer to the refrigerator to halt fermentation.

MAKES 1 PINT   Prep: **10 minutes** | Fermentation: **1 to 2 days** | Storage: **2 months**

Notes:

SEASONAL SWAP: *This recipe is highly malleable based on your personal preferences and what is available during the season. If you like, try adding different flavorings such as a sliced orange, lemon, or lime, several cardamom pods, a vanilla bean, or even a couple of dried chiles. Just be sure to stick with the ratio of honey, salt, whey, and berries, and use your imagination to go from there.*

FERMENTED TRI-BERRY SAUCE

Similar to fermented berries, this chunky berry sauce is great mixed with plain yogurt or served on top of waffles, pancakes, or ice cream. I enjoy the different textures and flavors of the berries blended together, but if you prefer just one, pick your favorite and make it with just that. This sauce stores well, so there is no rush to finish it—even though you may be tempted to eat it all in one sitting.

2 cups blackberries

1 cup raspberries

1 cup blueberries

¼ cup whey (page 31)

3 tablespoons sugar

½ teaspoon pickling salt

1 In a small bowl, mash the berries well to extract their juices, then pack the berries and their juices into a pint jar. In another bowl, combine the whey, sugar, and salt. Pour this mixture over the berries and add water to cover, if needed.

2 Cover the jar with a lid and let the berries ferment at room temperature for 48 hours. Transfer to the refrigerator to halt fermentation.

MAKES 1 PINT   Prep: **10 minutes** | Fermentation: **2 days** | Storage: **1 month**

Notes:

SEASONAL SWAP: *If you want to brighten your day in the dead of winter, this is your sauce. Happily, you can make it with frozen berries with no loss of quality or flavor. Just allow the berries to come to room temperature before mashing and adding the whey, sugar, and salt.*

LACTO-FERMENTED RASPBERRY-MINT SYRUP

There's nothing like homemade waffles or pancakes with a fresh fruit syrup in the summer. The bright, sweet flavor of raspberries plays out in amazing ways on your taste buds. Mint is a fantastic partner to raspberries and adds an element of complexity to this simple yet delectable syrup. When finished, it is mixed with maple syrup for a decadent, smooth sauce brimming with flavor.

4 cups raspberries
Leaves from 1 mint sprig
¼ cup whey (page 31)
¼ cup sugar
1½ teaspoons pickling salt
1 cup pure maple syrup

1 In a medium bowl, toss together the berries, mint, whey, sugar, and salt. Mash the berries well, and transfer to a quart jar. Cover the jar with a lid, and leave at room temperature for 2 days.

2 Using a stainless-steel mesh strainer and a funnel or jar filler, pour the contents of the jar into a clean pint jar, straining the pulp and seeds from the syrup. Allow the pulp to drain well, pressing gently to extract the liquid. You should have about 1 cup of liquid. Mix in the maple syrup, and refrigerate to halt fermentation.

MAKES 1 PINT   Prep: **10 minutes** | Fermentation: **2 days** | Storage: **2 months**

Notes:

SEASONAL SWAP: *Other herbs such as rosemary, cilantro, and basil can all work well in a syrup like this, depending on your tastes and what is available to you during the season. Substitute any of these for the mint in equal proportions. For a sumptuous vanilla-flavored treat, another alternative is to add a split, seeded vanilla bean to the raspberries while they ferment.*

FERMENTED BLACKBERRY-SAGE SYRUP

A taste explosion in the mouth, blackberry and sage are two flavors that were destined to be combined. Like the Lacto-Fermented Raspberry-Mint Syrup (page 99), this works well over waffles, pancakes, yogurt, or ice cream, and makes a great topping for a bowl of granola. If you think the combination sounds strange, try eating some blackberries with a couple of minced sage leaves sprinkled on top, and see what you think of this atypical pairing.

4 cups blackberries
10 sage leaves, torn
¼ cup whey (page 31)
¼ cup sugar
1½ teaspoons pickling salt
1 cup pure maple syrup

1 In a medium bowl, toss together the berries, sage, whey, sugar, and salt. Mash the berries well, and transfer the mixture to a quart jar. Cover the jar with a lid, and leave at room temperature for 2 days.

2 Using a stainless-steel mesh strainer and a funnel or jar filler, pour the contents of the jar into a clean pint jar, straining the pulp and seeds from the syrup. Allow the pulp to drain well, pressing gently to extract the liquid. You should have about 1 cup of liquid. Stir in the maple syrup and refrigerate to halt fermentation.

MAKES 1 PINT   Prep: **10 minutes** | Fermentation: **2 days** | Storage: **2 months**

Notes:

STRAWBERRY-MINT CHIA JAM

Chia seeds act like magic when making raw fermented jams. Upon contact with liquid, they swell up to create a gelatinous jam bursting with both character and nutrients. High in antioxidants, fiber, calcium, and heart-healthy omega-3 fatty acids, chia seeds are a winning ingredient. If you don't like the idea of a "spotty" jam, use a mortar and pestle, spice grinder, or clean coffee grinder to pulverize the seeds before using.

2½ cups strawberries,
   fresh or frozen

5 to 10 mint leaves, thinly sliced

¼ cup chia seeds

¼ cup raw honey

2 tablespoons whey (page 31)

½ teaspoon pickling salt

1 In a blender, purée the strawberries. Transfer to a small bowl and add the mint leaves, chia seeds, honey, whey, and pickling salt, stirring well to combine.

2 Transfer the jam to a pint jar and cover with a lid. Leave at room temperature for 24 to 48 hours. Transfer to the refrigerator to halt fermentation.

MAKES 1 PINT   Prep: **10 minutes** | Fermentation: **1 to 2 days** Storage: **1 month**

Notes:

A CLOSER LOOK: *Jams are a great place to flex your creativity. This type of chia jam can be reproduced using your favorite fruit in place of strawberries. Use equal proportions of fruit, honey, chia seeds, whey, and salt, but otherwise feel free to customize this to your tastes. Different herbs and flavorings such as lemon, vanilla, cilantro, basil, orange, lavender, and chiles can all make fun and flavorful additions to your own complex, personalized jams.*

JAM
TROUBLESHOOTING TIPS

Because the fermentation process is so short for jams, problems and mishaps are pretty rare. Most commonly, if something goes wrong, these are the culprits:

Jam became alcoholic. Fruits contain a lot of sugar, enabling the jump from lacto-fermentation to alcoholic fermentation. Keep fermentation time short to prevent this from taking place, and ensure that the temperature is not too high. Keep ferments in a cool location away from the kitchen, preferably around 72°F, especially in hotter months when speedy fermentation can occur.

Mold growth. If mold has grown on your ferment, chances are the temperature is too high. Also, like other ferments, it is important that the solids stay immersed in the liquids during fermentation. While this is a little tricky with a jam that becomes gelatinous, keep any larger chunks of fruit submerged in the jam to prevent mold from growing. For the best results, always use fresh fruit that has not been sitting around a long time before processing.

Too much liquid. The consistency of raw, fermented jams is a little different than that of cooked jams, which use pectin for firming. In recipes using chia seeds, the consistency is more like a store-bought jam, while other raw, fermented jams are a little looser. If you prefer a firmer jam, add 2 to 4 tablespoons of chia seeds to the jam before fermentation to thicken it.

LACTO-FERMENTED RASPBERRY-JALAPEÑO CHIA JAM

If you like the hot-sweet combination, then this is the jam for you. Thickened with chia seeds, this is a spreadable jam that is as good on toast or a biscuit as it is with crackers and cheese. The recipe calls for just one jalapeño, but if you have mild winter jalapeños, you might want to add an extra one (or two) to heat things up to just the right level.

3 cups raspberries, fresh or frozen

1 jalapeño, seeded and minced

¼ cup chia seeds

¼ cup raw honey

2 tablespoons whey (page 31)

½ teaspoon pickling salt

1 In a bowl, mash the raspberries well. Add the jalapeño, chia seeds, honey, whey, and salt, stirring well to combine.

2 Transfer the jam to a pint jar and cover with a lid. Leave at room temperature for 24 to 48 hours. Transfer to the refrigerator to halt fermentation.

MAKES 1 PINT   Prep: **10 minutes** | Fermentation: **1 to 2 days** | Storage: **1 month**

Notes:

A CLOSER LOOK: *Chia seeds, like pectin in more traditional jam making, take a while to become activated for gelling. They must first absorb some water and become hydrated before they can firm up the texture of your jam, so don't expect firmness immediately upon mixing. Come back in a couple of hours and give the jar a little shake. By then they should be well hydrated and producing the thick texture you desire.*

LACTO-FERMENTED RASPBERRY-LAVENDER JAM

When I ran a company selling artisanal jams at a farmers' market, this was one of my customers' favorite combinations. While I didn't ferment that jam because it was canned, this one is comparable, including both a probiotic boost and the health benefits of chia. Be sure to use food-grade lavender that has not been treated with chemicals.

1 tablespoon fresh lavender flowers

¼ cup boiling water

¼ cup chia seeds, ground

3 cups raspberries, fresh or frozen

¼ cup raw honey

2 tablespoons whey (page 31)

½ teaspoon pickling salt

1 In a small bowl, combine the lavender flowers and boiling water. Cover and steep for 30 minutes. Strain the water, discarding the lavender flowers. Transfer 2 tablespoons of the lavender water to a small bowl. Add the ground chia seeds to the bowl and stir well.

2 In another bowl, mash the raspberries and mix in the honey, whey, and salt.

3 Once the lavender water–chia mixture begins to slightly congeal, stir it into the raspberry mixture, and transfer to a pint jar. Cover with a lid and leave at room temperature for 2 days. Transfer to the refrigerator to halt fermentation.

MAKES 1 PINT

Prep: **10 minutes** | Rest: **40 minutes** | Fermentation: **2 days** | Storage: **1 month**

Notes:

A CLOSER LOOK: *For this recipe, I steep a tablespoon of fresh flowers to make a strongly flavored lavender water. However, because we use only about half of this for the jam, make a double batch—or do as I do, and use this floral water to flavor lemonade or other vinegars or sweets.*

FERMENTED BLACKBERRY JAM

As blackberries contain a lot of pectin, fresh jams made from these sweet berries are naturally a lot firmer. Here, just a spoonful of ground chia seeds is added to create a thicker jam on par with store-bought varieties for spreadability. This simple jam is just begging to top your toast and brighten your meal. If you prefer, boysenberries are equally wonderful in a natural fruit jam like this.

2½ cups blackberries,
   fresh or frozen
¼ cup raw honey
2 tablespoons whey (page 31)
1 tablespoon ground chia seeds
½ teaspoon pickling salt

1 In a small bowl, mash the blackberries well. Mix in the honey, whey, chia seeds, and salt.

2 Transfer to a pint jar, cover, and ferment at room temperature for 2 days. Transfer to the refrigerator to halt fermentation.

MAKES 1 PINT Prep: **5 minutes** | Fermentation: **2 days** | Storage: **1 month**

Notes:

FERMENTED APRICOT JAM

This simple spread uses dried apricots, which saves considerably on preparation time and allows you to make this any time of year. Be sure to check the label and select unsulfured apricots to promote a healthy fermentation. By the time the apricots have finished fermenting, you'll have a well-thickened spread that tastes like summer.

1 cup dried apricots
2 tablespoons whey (page 31)
2 tablespoons raw honey
½ teaspoon pickling salt

1 Put the apricots in a small saucepan and cover with water. Bring the water to a boil over medium-high heat, turn down the heat, and simmer until the apricots are tender, about 30 minutes. Drain the water and transfer the apricots to a blender. Process until smooth, transfer to a small bowl, and let cool to room temperature.

2 Mix in the whey, honey, and salt. Transfer to a pint jar, cover with a lid, and leave to ferment for 2 days. Transfer to the refrigerator to halt fermentation.

MAKES 1 PINT

Prep: **5 minutes** | Cook: **30 minutes** | Fermentation: **2 days** | Storage: **1 month**

Notes:

LACTO-FERMENTED SPICED ORANGE MARMALADE

Orange marmalade is a bright, fruity spread that shines with hints of cinnamon and clove. This simple recipe uses ground chia seeds to aid in thickening, creating a marmalade that rounds up on a spoon just like a commercial one. Because the rind is used as well, organic oranges are recommended.

4 medium-size organic oranges

¼ cup water

1 cinnamon stick

3 whole cloves

1 (1-inch) piece ginger, peeled and sliced

2 tablespoons raw honey

2 tablespoons whey (page 31)

2 tablespoons ground chia seeds

1 teaspoon salt

1 Quarter and peel the oranges and mince the peels. In a small saucepan, combine half of the oranges and peels with the water, cinnamon, cloves, and ginger and bring the mixture to a boil over medium-high heat. Reduce the heat and cook for about 1 hour over low heat.

2 Chop the remaining oranges into small pieces and mix them in a small bowl with the remaining peels. Add the honey and whey, stir well, and set aside.

3 After an hour of cooking, remove the saucepan from the burner and add the ground chia seeds and salt. Stir well and cool to room temperature. Once cool, combine the raw and cooked orange mixtures and pack into a clean pint jar. Affix a lid and let the jam ferment at room temperature for 3 days. Transfer to the refrigerator to halt fermentation.

MAKES 1 PINT

Prep: **15 minutes** | Rest: **30 minutes** | Cook: **1 hour** | Fermentation: **3 days** | Storage: **1 month**

- -

Notes:

- -

SEASONAL SWAP: *For a slightly sweeter jam, try using a smaller, sweeter variety of orange, such as clementine or tangerine. These are available in many markets throughout the winter months.*

FERMENTED APPLE BUTTER

This spreadable condiment is delicious on a piece of crusty bread, but it also can be turned into a fabulous sauce for poultry and pork dishes. Make this recipe in a slow cooker for a hands-off project that requires very little active time in the kitchen. And the best part? The irresistible aroma of apple butter that takes over your house as it cooks.

3 pounds apples
½ cup water
1 tablespoon ground cinnamon
1 teaspoon ground nutmeg
2 tablespoons whey (page 31)

1 Peel, core, and quarter the apples. Cut them into a chunky dice and place them in a slow cooker. Add the water, cinnamon, and nutmeg. Cover and cook on low for 6 to 8 hours. Using an immersion blender, food processor, or blender, purée the apples and return them to the slow cooker.

2 Continue to cook the apples on low in the slow cooker, but keep the lid propped open to allow the steam to escape and the apple butter to cook down. After 1 hour, check the consistency. It should be thick enough to stay on a spoon for a second or two when tipped to the side. When it is ready, transfer the apple butter to a quart jar. Cool to room temperature, then stir in the whey.

3 Cover the jar with a lid and leave at room temperature for 2 days. Transfer to the refrigerator to halt fermentation.

MAKES 1 QUART

Prep: **10 minutes** | Slow-Cook: **7 to 9 hours** | Fermentation: **2 days** | Storage: **2 months**

Notes:

A CLOSER LOOK: *To take your apple butter a step further, consider making fruit leathers. This healthy alternative to commercially available fruit leathers is a snap to make if you have a dehydrator, but it is also possible to make it in the oven. Set your oven to its lowest setting and line a baking sheet with a piece of parchment paper. Spoon a generous cup of apple butter onto the sheet and use the back of a spoon to spread it around so that it's about ¼ inch thick. Place it in the oven and cook until it hardens and becomes nearly dried, 1 to 2 hours. Remove the sheet from the oven and let cool before slicing the fruit leather into individual servings.*

FERMENTED PEAR BUTTER

Anytime I can throw something in the slow cooker and create a product as good as one made on the stove, I do. Like apple butter, this recipe is supremely simple. As a bonus, you get to enjoy the spiced pear aroma all day long. When it's done, slather it on a piece of toast and savor the richness of fall flavor at its finest.

3 pounds pears
½ cup water
1 tablespoon ground cinnamon
1½ teaspoons ground ginger
2 tablespoons whey (page 31)

1 Peel, core, and quarter the pears. Cut them into a chunky dice and place them in the slow cooker. Add the water, cinnamon, and ginger. Cover and cook on low for 6 to 8 hours. Using an immersion blender, food processor, or blender, purée the pears and return them to the slow cooker.

2 Continue to cook the pears on low in the slow cooker, with the lid propped open to allow the steam to escape and the pear butter to cook down. After 1 hour, check the consistency. It should be thick enough to stay on a spoon for a second or two when it is tipped to the side. When it is ready, after 1 to 2 hours, transfer the pear butter to a quart jar. Cool to room temperature, and then stir in the whey.

3 Cover the jar with a lid and leave at room temperature for 2 days. Transfer to the refrigerator to halt fermentation.

MAKES 1 QUART

Prep: **10 minutes** | Cook: **7 to 9 hours** | Fermentation: **2 days** | Storage: **2 months**

Notes:

A CLOSER LOOK: *Because the pears cook down so much when making this recipe, it is quite sweet when finished, so don't be tempted to add sugar before trying the final product. If at the end of cooking you still feel it needs a little sweetness, add a spoonful or two of brown sugar to sweeten it slightly.*

SPICED FERMENTED APPLES

I am the first to admit that when I first heard of fermenting apples, I thought the practice was crazy. However, over the years this complex pickled fruit has grown on me considerably. For the best flavor, start with apples that are already quite sweet, such as Honeycrisp or Gala, which both ferment well. Don't put this ferment in a corner and forget about it. In some cases, this ferment will be finished in just 4 days.

3 medium-size apples

4 cinnamon sticks, crushed

Grated zest of 1 lemon,
   plus 1 tablespoon lemon juice

2 tablespoons pickling salt

3 cups water

1 Quarter and core the apples. Slice thinly by hand, using the slicing disk on a food processor or a mandoline. Create a brine by mixing the cinnamon, lemon zest, lemon juice, and salt into the water and stirring until the salt is dissolved.

2 Pack the apples into a quart jar. Pour the brine over the apples to cover, and weight down the apples with a small weight. Cover the jar with a clean kitchen towel secured by a rubber band. Leave at room temperature for 4 to 7 days. Begin testing the apples at 4 days, and when they are well soured, transfer to the refrigerator to halt fermentation.

MAKES 1 QUART   Prep: **10 minutes** | Fermentation: **4 to 7 days** | Storage: **3 months**

Notes:

FERMENTED APPLE PICKLES

This recipe uses whey, which adds its own distinct flavor to a ferment. While pickled apples are not for everyone, they're easy to make and completely unique in flavor. This recipe is a fun project to do with kids, as they tend to find the transformation of an apple fascinating.

3 medium-size apples
1½ tablespoons pickling salt
2 tablespoons whey (page 31)

1 Peel, quarter, and core the apples. Slice thinly by hand, using the slicing disk on a food processor or a mandoline. In a large bowl, toss the apples with the salt to coat.

2 Pack the apples into a quart jar. Pour the whey over the apples, and then top off with enough water to cover but still leave 1 inch of headspace. Weight the apples down with a small weight. Cover the jar with a clean kitchen towel secured by a rubber band, and leave at room temperature for 1 to 3 days. If it tastes good after 1 day, it's finished. If not, continue to ferment for up to 2 more days, then transfer to the refrigerator to halt fermentation.

MAKES 1 QUART   Prep: **10 minutes** | Fermentation: **1 to 3 days** | Storage: **3 months**

Notes:

FERMENTED CHERRIES

If you are looking for an adults-only fermented cherry, this is your recipe. The hardest part is waiting a month to eat these beauties. While they will last for up to 1 year, the chances of that happening are slim to none. When the cherries are all gone, enjoy the resulting port-like leftover liquid.

8 ounces firm, red cherries, pitted
½ cup sugar
½ cup water
¼ cup brandy

1 Using a toothpick, poke each cherry several times, down to the pit. Pack the cherries into a pint jar, leaving 1 inch of headspace.

2 In a saucepan, cook the sugar and water over medium-high heat, stirring to dissolve the sugar. Continue to simmer until a thin syrup forms, about 10 minutes. Pour the hot syrup over the cherries, and top off the jar with the brandy. Secure a top loosely in place, and leave the cherries to ferment at room temperature for 2 weeks to 1 month, shaking the jar about once a week. When bubbles stop rising in the jar, the cherries are done. Transfer to the refrigerator for storage.

MAKES 1 PINT   Prep: **20 minutes** | Fermentation: **2 weeks to 1 month** | Storage: **1 year**

Notes:

FERMENTED PLUMS

Fermented plums are a soured, pickled treat that you must try to understand. This recipe is inspired by the Japanese umeboshi. Though umeboshi literally translates to "pickled plum," they are actually a type of apricot unavailable in the United States. I suggest you select smaller varieties like Italian plums and choose those that are underripe and still hard. If you know someone with a plum tree in their yard, this is a great way to get plums at just the right time—after they have turned color, but before they have softened.

1½ pounds underripe plums
¼ cup pickling salt
2 cups water

1 Prick the surface of the plums several times. Pack the plums into a quart jar.

2 Dissolve the salt in the water, and pour this brine over the plums. Weight the plums down using a small weight. Do not top off the jar with additional water, as the plums will produce a lot of juice over the next few days.

3 Leave at room temperature for 3 weeks. Transfer to the refrigerator, and allow the plums to cure for up to 1 month before eating.

MAKES 1 QUART

Prep: **10 minutes** | Fermentation: **3 weeks, plus 1 month curing** | Storage: **1 year**

Notes:

MAKE IT A MEAL: *In Japan, this type of pickled plum is served with rice for a light meal. If you want something quick and easy, try eating one or two sliced plums with a small bowl of rice. The plums can also be sliced up and added to a variety of Asian and Western-style dishes to create an intense umami flavor.*

FERMENTED PEACH SPREAD

Peaches are one of my favorite fruits of summer, and this simple spread captures their essence particularly well. Cook the pulp down until it is thick and nearly a fruit butter, stopping at the point when it is still pourable. Serve it over ice cream, slather it on toast, or pair it with cream cheese and crackers.

2 pounds peaches, peeled, pitted, and coarsely chopped

½ cup raw honey

2 tablespoons whey (page 31)

1 teaspoon pickling salt

1 Place the peaches in a small saucepan and lightly mash them to release their juices. Bring them to a boil over medium-high heat, then reduce the heat to a simmer. Simmer, stirring occasionally, until the plums are broken down and the liquid is reduced by one-third to one-half of its volume, 1 to 3 hours. The sauce should still be pourable but not runny. Cool to room temperature.

2 Mix in the honey, whey, and salt. Transfer to a pint jar, cover with a lid, and ferment at room temperature for 2 days. Transfer to the refrigerator to halt fermentation.

MAKES 1 PINT

Prep: **15 minutes** | Cook: **1 to 3 hours** | Fermentation: **2 days** | Storage: **2 months**

- -

Notes:

- -

SEASONAL SWAP: *Make this same spread with nectarines, plums, or other stone fruits if you miss peaches this season. For added complexity, add a sprig of rosemary to the fermenting fruit.*

LACTO-FERMENTED CHERRY SALSA

If you ever have an excess of cherries, a great way to preserve them is by making this salsa. Once fermented, it will keep for a couple of months in the fridge, outlasting its fresh counterpart by miles. Because it is not cooked like many salsas bound for canning, it will stay crisp and won't turn to mush.

1 pound dark, sweet cherries, stemmed and pitted

½ cup chopped fresh cilantro

¼ cup chopped fresh mint

2 cups chopped scallions

2 serrano peppers, seeded if desired and minced

¼ cup freshly squeezed lemon juice

¼ cup whey (page 31)

1 tablespoon sugar

2 teaspoons pickling salt

1 In a large bowl, toss all of the ingredients together. Pack the salsa into a quart jar, leaving 1 inch of headspace, and affix the lid.

2 Leave at room temperature to ferment for 1 to 2 days, and then transfer to the refrigerator to halt fermentation.

MAKES 1 QUART   Prep: **10 minutes** | Fermentation: **1 to 2 days** | Storage: **2 to 3 months**

Notes:

SEASONAL SWAP: *If you can't find dark cherries, Rainier cherries can also be used for this delicious salsa. With a slightly different flavor, these still pack in plenty of sweetness and make a beautiful yellow and red salsa flooded with color.*

LACTO-FERMENTED VANILLA PEACHES

If you ever have an excess of cherries, a great way to preserve them is by making this salsa. Once fermented, it will keep for a couple of months in the fridge, outlasting its fresh counterpart by miles. Because it is not cooked like many salsas bound for canning, it will stay crisp and won't turn to mush.

4 cups diced, peeled peaches
1 teaspoon pickling salt
1 vanilla bean, split lengthwise

1 In a small bowl, combine the peaches and salt.

2 Pack the peaches into a quart jar, pressing down as you go to remove air bubbles. Ensure there is at least 2 inches of headspace in the jar.

3 Insert the vanilla bean into the jar, placing one piece on each side of the jar below the surface of the peaches.

4 Cover with a nonreactive lid. Place in a room temperature location for 12 to 24 hours. If your house is warmer than 72°F, 12 hours is recommended. When fermentation is complete, remove the vanilla bean, and transfer the jar to the refrigerator for storage.

MAKES 1 QUART   Prep: **10 minutes** | Fermentation: **12 to 24 hours** | Storage: **3 weeks**

Notes:

CHAPTER SIX

Dairy

Not that long ago, and still in some places today, fermentation was the only way to preserve milk when refrigeration was unavailable. Developed as a means of preservation, dairy fermentation has brought us culinary cornerstones like cheese and yogurt. Using some of the same simple, time-tested techniques of the original fermenters who developed these foods out of necessity, you can practice this age-old process in your own home to produce dairy ferments like kefir, yogurt, sour cream, and buttermilk with great results.

Recipes

DAIRY FERMENTATION BASICS

If you feel intimidated by the thought of fermenting dairy, don't worry. While dairy fermentation is not yet a mainstream activity in the United States, people around the world use these techniques day in and day out.

Getting Prepared

• **Start with good milk.** Full-fat milk is the best option, but if you prefer low-fat, that will work, too. Do not use nonfat (skim) milk, though, as it does not work as well for fermenting. Pasteurized milk is great, but avoid all types of ultra-high temperature (UHT) pasteurized milk—the kind usually sold in aseptic boxes on the supermarket shelves—as these are not suitable for fermentation. Organic milk from pastured cows is the best choice, both for avoiding hormones and because it contains a higher vitamin content. If you like, you can also use goat's milk for the recipes in this chapter.

• **Ratios are key.** When it comes to dairy fermentation, there isn't much wiggle room for ratios. Be careful not to change the proportions of ingredients in any of these recipes, as they may not turn out as expected if you do. If you are making a secondary ferment of kefir or flavoring yogurts, it's fine to play around with proportions, but be sure that you have the initial fermentation process down before you go veering off the recipe.

The Fermentation Process

• **Set it, but don't forget it.** For most dairy ferments, once the initial process is done, your active work is complete and nature takes its course. Take note not to stash your ferments somewhere you will not see them regularly, as this is a good way to ruin a ferment. Keep them in view to remind you that you are working on them.

• **Test and test often.** Dairy ferments like yogurt and kefir can change considerably in a short period of time. Be careful to keep a close eye on them, and do not let them ferment for longer than indicated in the recipe. Test them with a clean utensil every few hours until you get the hang of it and know what to expect.

Dairy

KEFIR
TROUBLESHOOTING TIPS

Kefir is pretty straightforward and simple, especially once your grains are going well. As long as you keep them fed regularly with new milk, they will work hard for you for a long time. Every once in a while, though, even the most diligent kefir maker runs into problems. Here are some of the most common problems and their solutions.

Curds are separating from whey. This begins to happen when the grains are working so hard that they over-ferment the kefir. To prevent this, you have several options. You can increase the amount of milk you are fermenting or decrease the amount of grains you are using. You can also decrease the fermentation time and lower the temperature during fermentation.

Kefir is too thick. When the curds separate from the whey, this can make it difficult to strain the kefir. If this occurs (which it eventually will if you make kefir for long), simply mix the curds and whey back together by vigorously stirring the kefir. Strain as usual, using the back of a spoon to force the larger curds through the strainer.

Kefir smells yeasty. This is pretty common and should not concern you. However, if the kefir smells like yeast of the rotten variety, it should be tossed.

Kefir is not thickening. If you are using fully rehydrated grains and the kefir is not thickening, try reducing the quantity of milk used by ½ cup until the milk thickens well within 24 hours. You can always begin fermenting more milk again, but do not try to ferment more than 4 cups of milk per 2 tablespoons of grains.

Kefir is moldy. Mold is rather uncommon in kefir but can sometimes occur. Do not throw away a batch of kefir simply because it looks funny. Kefir grains can be a yellowish color, and it would be a shame to toss perfectly good grains for nothing. Mold can be pink, black, brown, yellow, or green. If you are in doubt, consult the Internet for a better idea of what mold looks like on kefir. If it is indeed mold, toss the batch and start again with new grains.

starter recipe KEFIR

MAKES 1 PINT Prep: **5 minutes** | Fermentation: **24 hours** | Storage: **5 days**

Kefir is a great beginner fermentation project because it requires very little work. In the end, you are left with a soured product that makes delicious probiotic smoothies—and works equally well when cooking as a stand-in for milk, buttermilk, or yogurt. Unlike many other ferments that do perfectly well on the counter covered with a clean kitchen cloth, kefir is particularly prone to contamination. For this reason, I recommend using a lid to cover the jar during fermentation to prevent cross-contamination with other ferments in your kitchen.

2 tablespoons rehydrated kefir grains
2 cups milk

1 Put the kefir grains in a pint jar.

2 Pour the milk over the grains and close the jar loosely with a nonreactive lid.

continues ▶

Home Fermentation

3 Leave the jar at room temperature for 24 hours, or until the milk becomes visibly thickened.

4 Using a stainless-steel mesh strainer and a funnel or jar filler, pour the kefir into the clean jar, reserving the grains in the strainer. Depending on the size of your strainer, you may have to work in batches. If the kefir does not strain freely through the strainer, stir it gently with a spoon to speed up the process.

5 Put the kefir grains in a new jar, and begin again. Store the finished kefir in a covered jar, and keep refrigerated.

Notes:

A CLOSER LOOK: *Kefir grains require fresh milk to stay active. When you are ready to take a break from kefir making, put your kefir grains in a jar with fresh milk, close the jar with a lid, and refrigerate the jar for up to 1 week before replacing the milk. While this is an effective method for keeping your kefir grains active, it should be used only when you are unable to ferment, not as a regular practice. If you do not drink a lot of kefir, consider making a small batch daily, instead of making a larger batch and refrigerating the grains in between.*

RASPBERRY-MINT KEFIR

Secondary fermentation increases the probiotic benefits of kefir and can also increase the carbonation, leaving you with a fizzy, delicious treat. A handheld immersion blender makes this project a breeze, but if you don't have one, a traditional countertop blender or food processor can be used in its place.

1½ cups Kefir (page 125)
¼ cup raspberries
4 or 5 mint leaves

1 Combine the kefir, raspberries, and mint leaves in a pint jar. Using an immersion blender, purée the raspberries and mint into the kefir.

2 Cover the jar with a lid and leave at room temperature for 12 hours. Refrigerate or serve immediately.

MAKES 1 PINT   Prep: **5 minutes** | Fermentation: **12 hours** | Storage: **3 to 5 days**

Notes:

A CLOSER LOOK: *Secondary fermenting kefir with fruit can make it very effervescent, which I personally love. If you prefer your kefir to be smooth instead of bubbly, you can instead allow for secondary fermentation of the kefir with just the mint, and then purée the raspberries in at the end after that process is complete.*

REHYDRATING KEFIR GRAINS

If you buy dried kefir grains from a commercial retailer, you will need to rehydrate them when you get them home. This simple process requires about 7 days but very little work.

To rehydrate kefir grains, empty the contents of the package into a pint jar, add 1 cup cold pasteurized milk, cover the jar with a lid, and place in a location between 68° and 85°F. After 24 hours, strain the grains from the milk and transfer them to another jar with a fresh cup of milk. Continue this process until the milk thickens within 24 hours. When this occurs, increase the amount of milk by ½ cup daily until you reach 4 cups (at 2 cups, transfer to a quart jar). When you are at 4 cups and the milk thickens within 24 hours, the grains are fully rehydrated. After the milk begins to thicken the first time (at 1 cup), it is fine to drink the kefir, though it may not produce the best flavor until the grains are fully hydrated.

ORANGE-SPICED KEFIR

One of the benefits of secondary fermentation is that it creates a smoother, mellowed kefir. There is no better example than this simple mixture that draws its flavor from orange peel. Be sure to use an organic orange for this, and cut only the outer zest, not the bitter white pith from the inside of the peel.

2 cups Kefir (page 125)
Peel from ½ orange
½ teaspoon grated ginger
1 cinnamon stick

1 Combine the kefir, orange peel, ginger, and cinnamon stick in a pint jar. Cover the jar with a lid and leave at room temperature for 12 hours.

2 Remove the orange peel and cinnamon stick from the kefir. Refrigerate or serve immediately.

MAKES 1 PINT Prep: **5 minutes** | Fermentation: **12 hours** | Storage: **3 to 5 days**

Notes:

A CLOSER LOOK: *It can be difficult to tell when kefir is ready, especially by sight. One of the best indications is when the liquid and whey start to separate in the bottom of the jar. Try to place the finished kefir in the refrigerator just around the time this begins, as letting it continue to ferment will cause it to separate more. To recombine the two, simply stir the whey back into the kefir.*

KEFIR CHEESE

This simple cheese is great added to salads and soups, or mixed with herbs to spread on crackers or sandwiches. The best time to make this is when you accidently over-ferment your kefir and it separates into curds and whey. As always, be sure to save the whey to use in other ferments in this book.

4 cups Kefir (page 125)

1 Line a large colander with a few layers of cheesecloth and set it over a large bowl. Pour the kefir into the colander, and transfer the bowl and colander to the refrigerator.

2 Let the kefir drain for up to 24 hours, until all that is left in the colander are the thick curds. Gather the cheesecloth together at the edges and press the curds into a firm ball. Store in a covered container in the refrigerator until ready to serve.

MAKES 1 CUP   Prep: **5 minutes** | Draining: **12 to 24 hours** | Storage: **1 week**

Notes:

A CLOSER LOOK: *For a plain cheese, add up to 1 teaspoon kosher salt; for more flavor, add chopped sage, basil, or thyme to the cheese. If you are adding seasonings, mix them with the cheese first, and then gather the cheese in the cheesecloth to form it into a ball.*

STRAWBERRY-LAVENDER KEFIR

Home Fermentation

Lavender is an unusual seasoning, as most people seem to associate it merely with perfume. If the thought of drinking a flower doesn't appeal to you, you are not alone. However, I hope you will give this one a try. Fruit and lavender make a great pairing, and it suits kefir wonderfully. Taste it and see what you think.

½ cup strawberries

1¾ cups Kefir (page 125)

1 teaspoon dried food-grade lavender flowers, secured in a spice pouch or tied up in a scrap of cheesecloth

Honey (optional)

1 In a blender, purée the strawberries. Transfer to a pint jar, add the kefir, and stir well. Add the spice pouch with lavender and affix the lid. Leave at room temperature for 12 hours.

2 Remove and discard lavender flower spice pouch, screw on the lid, and transfer the kefir to the refrigerator; when ready to serve, sweeten with honey as desired.

MAKES 1 PINT Prep: **5 minutes** | Fermentation: **12 hours** | Storage: **3 to 5 days**

Notes:

VEGGIE KEFIR

Most recipes for kefir are sweet, and that's fine, but I am more of a savory person. This recipe provides a great alternative secondary fermentation of kefir combined with the flavors of a full-bodied vegetable juice. Find vegetable powders online or at specialty stores—or, if you have a dehydrator, make your own.

2 cups Kefir (page 125)
¼ cup tomato powder
1 tablespoon green pepper powder
1 tablespoon celery powder

1 Combine the kefir and vegetable powders in a pint jar. Cover the jar with a lid and leave at room temperature for 12 hours.

2 Refrigerate or serve immediately.

Dairy

MAKES 1 PINT   Prep: **5 minutes** | Fermentation: **12 hours** | Storage: **3 to 5 days**

Notes:

A CLOSER LOOK: *Vegetable powders are easy to make and can be a great way to use otherwise discarded pieces of vegetables like tomatoes. When canning, I typically blanch tomatoes to remove their skins. Before I knew about tomato powder, I would just throw away the skins. Now I dehydrate them at 110°F for 12 to 14 hours, and they become crisp and crunchy. Grind these in a spice grinder or with a mortar and pestle, and you have a virtually free powder for seasoning kefir and other foods.*

YOGURT

Yogurt requires a bit more oversight and time than kefir, but it's well worth the effort. Slightly thinner, smoother, and tangier than its store-bought counterpart, homemade yogurt is delicious mixed with granola, fruit, or a drizzle of honey. You will need a small insulated cooler or lunch bag to make this, as well as a candy thermometer. Because it takes a little longer to prepare, I prefer to make at least a quart per batch to save time in the kitchen.

4 cups milk

2 tablespoons commercial plain yogurt with live cultures

1   In a thick-bottomed pot, heat the milk to 200°F over medium heat, stirring it regularly to prevent scorching and boiling over. As soon as the temperature reaches 200°F, turn off the heat and remove the pan from the stove.

2   Cool the milk to 115° F. You can either let the milk cool on its own or immerse the pot in an ice water bath to speed up the process. Either way, stir the milk as it cools to prevent a skin from forming on its surface.

3   Using a ladle, remove some of the warm milk from the pot, and add the yogurt to the ladle. Mix it well to thin the yogurt, and add this back to the pot of warm milk.

4   Pour the yogurt into a quart jar and close the lid tightly. Place the jar in an insulated cooler. Fill an additional quart jar or pint jar with hot water (as hot as your sink will go) and cap this jar. Place this in the cooler next to the milk. Close the cooler and leave for up to 12 hours, until the yogurt sets.

5   Check the yogurt every few hours to determine if it has set. If the yogurt and hot water jar are cool to the touch, refill the water jar with hot water. Once the yogurt is set, refrigerate it until cold before serving.

6   Save 2 tablespoons of the yogurt for a future batch, and start over again.

MAKES 1 QUART   Prep: **15 minutes** | Fermentation: **12 to 24 hours** | Storage: **2 weeks**

- -

Notes:

- -

A CLOSER LOOK: *You can make yogurt with nonfat or 1 percent milk, but I recommend whole or 2 percent milk. These produce yogurt with the creamiest texture and richest flavor.*

GREEK YOGURT

If you find the traditional yogurt (page 134) too loose for you, try this version instead. Greek yogurt tastes best when made with full-fat yogurt. Be sure to save your leftover whey for use in other fermenting projects.

4 cups Yogurt (page 134)

1 Line a strainer with several layers of cheesecloth and set it over a bowl. Pour the yogurt into the strainer and transfer the bowl and strainer to the refrigerator.

2 Once the whey has drained out into the bowl and the yogurt has thickened substantially, spoon the yogurt into a clean quart jar.

MAKES 2 TO 3 CUPS   Prep: **15 minutes** | Draining: **12 to 24 hours** | Storage: **7 days**

Notes:

BERRY YOGURT

Berry yogurt is perhaps one of the best tastes of summer. This recipe is quite simple to make, and easy to customize based on what's in season, allowing you to skip the yogurt aisle at the grocery store for good. Avoiding high-fructose corn syrup and other additives found in commercial varieties, this natural blend is fruit forward and still immensely sweet. Any berries work well in yogurt, but my favorites are blueberries, blackberries, and raspberries.

1 cup Yogurt (page 134)
3 cups mixed berries
1 tablespoon honey

In a blender, combine the yogurt, berries, and honey and process until smooth. Chill and serve.

MAKES 3 CUPS   Prep: **10 minutes** | Storage: **2 weeks**

Notes:

A CLOSER LOOK: *Use any mixture of fresh or frozen berries to make this simple, fruity yogurt. To freeze berries, spread them in a single layer on a baking sheet and freeze until solid. Once solid, pack the berries into a resealable bag and freeze for up to 1 year.*

CULTURED BUTTERMILK

There are two types of buttermilk: cultured buttermilk and the buttermilk left over from the butter-making process. While cultured buttermilk is not the traditional method from which buttermilk got its name, it makes a heck of a delicious waffle, biscuit, or pancake. Be sure the buttermilk you start with contains live cultures and no additives.

3 cups milk

1 cup commercial buttermilk

1 Combine the milk and buttermilk in a quart jar. Cover with a clean kitchen towel secured by a rubber band. Let it sit at room temperature for 12 to 24 hours, until it is thick and creamy and develops a tangy smell.

2 Seal the jar with a nonreactive lid and refrigerate. Always reserve 1 cup of the buttermilk for making subsequent batches.

MAKES 1 QUART   Prep: **15 minutes** | Fermentation: **12 to 24 hours** | Storage: **2 to 3 weeks**

Notes:

A CLOSER LOOK: *If you prefer to start with a commercial culture instead of buttermilk, purchase a direct-set buttermilk starter culture and add it to 4 cups of milk, following the same directions as above. This is a good option for those who don't have access to commercial buttermilk with live cultures.*

SOUR CREAM

Surprisingly, sour cream is quite easy to make. No fancy starter cultures here—all you need is heavy cream and a bit of cultured buttermilk. You'll never have to buy it again once you know this simple recipe. Just be sure to get it going well in advance so it has plenty of time to thicken and chill before you use it. Serve this tangy sour cream on tacos, add it to baked goods, or use it to make your favorite dip.

1 cup heavy cream
¼ cup Cultured Buttermilk
  (page 138)

1 Combine the heavy cream and cultured buttermilk in a pint jar. Cover with a clean kitchen towel secured by a rubber band. Let it sit at room temperature for 24 to 36 hours, until it is thick.

2 Seal the jar with a nonreactive lid and refrigerate. Reserve ½ cup of this sour cream each time you make it, for producing subsequent batches, and substitute it for the cultured buttermilk.

MAKES 1¼ CUPS Prep: **5 minutes** | Fermentation: **24 to 36 hours** | Storage: **1 week**

Notes:

A CLOSER LOOK: *If you want to make a low-fat sour cream, substitute up to half of the heavy cream with whole milk. Do not, however, try to use any milk lower than full-fat, as the sour cream will have a difficult time setting.*

CHÈVRE

Goat's milk has a distinctive flavor that most people either love or hate. I am definitely a full-fledged member of the love camp, and this is one of my favorite ways to use it. Bursting with flavor and funk, there is really nothing like goat cheese and pickled strawberries on a cracker. When left unseasoned, this soft, spreadable cheese pairs well with both sweet and savory foods, and it is beyond easy to make. Just take note that you will need a candy thermometer to accurately gauge the temperature of the milk.

1 gallon goat's milk
1 package direct-set chèvre culture
2 teaspoons cheese salt

1 In a large pot, warm the milk to 86°F over medium heat. Immediately remove the pot from the burner. Sprinkle the chèvre culture over the milk and allow it to rehydrate for a few minutes before stirring it into the milk.

2 Cover the pot with a clean kitchen towel and let it sit at room temperature for 12 hours to allow the curds to coagulate. Whey will form over the curds.

3 Line a colander with a triple layer of cheesecloth and set the colander over a large bowl. Transfer the mixture in the pot to the colander and drain the whey for about 6 hours. For a drier cheese, continue draining for up to 16 more hours.

4 Mix the cheese with the salt in a small bowl, cover, and store in the refrigerator.

MAKES 1 CUP

Prep: **5 minutes** | Rest time: **12 hours** | Draining: **6 to 24 hours** | Storage: **7 to 10 days**

Notes:

SEASONAL SWAP: *Add herbs to the chèvre based on the season (or your preferences) to enhance its flavor further. Garlic, parsley, sage, cilantro, rosemary, or basil can create a wonderful herbed cheese that tastes terrific with crackers or bread.*

CRÈME FRAÎCHE

Skip the high cost of artisan crème fraîche and save a trip to the grocery store by making it at home. You might notice that the ingredients and process are nearly identical to that of sour cream, the only differences being fermentation time and the ratio of cream to buttermilk. Crème fraîche has a slightly looser, more pourable consistency than sour cream. Spoon this treat over waffles, pancakes, or cakes, or add it to sauces and soups to thicken the texture and bump up the flavor.

1 cup heavy cream

2 tablespoons Cultured Buttermilk (page 138)

1 Combine the cream and buttermilk in a pint jar. Cover with a clean kitchen towel and let sit at room temperature for 12 hours, or until slightly thickened.

2 Seal the jar with a nonreactive lid and store in the refrigerator.

MAKES 1 CUP   Prep: **5 minutes** | Fermenting: **12 hours** | Storage: **1 week**

Notes:

CULTURED BUTTER WITH HERBS

Making butter can be a rewarding process, and culturing the cream first makes it an even tastier one. You need no fancy supplies, just a bit of plain kefir from a batch you've already made. In this recipe, I outline the directions using a mixer, but you can also make butter by hand using the technique described in the tip following the recipe. This is a great tactile project for kids, as they tend to be fascinated by the process.

2 cups heavy cream
2 tablespoons Kefir (page 125)
1 tablespoon minced garlic
1 tablespoon chopped fresh parsley
¼ teaspoon fine sea salt

1 Combine the cream and kefir in a pint jar. Cover with a clean kitchen towel and ferment at room temperature for 24 hours.

2 Transfer the cream to the freezer for 1 to 2 hours so it's very cold. Pour it into the bowl of a stand mixer and turn the mixer to the highest speed possible without splattering. Once the cream begins to thicken, increase the speed to high, monitoring closely.

3 Once the butter begins pulling apart from the buttermilk, reduce the speed to enable the butter to clump together.

4 Transfer the butter to a small bowl. Wash it by filling the bowl with filtered water and pressing out any remaining buttermilk with a silicone spatula. When the water runs clear, the butter is ready.

5 In a small bowl, mix the garlic, parsley, and sea salt into the butter until incorporated. With a small piece of wax paper wrapped around it, shape the butter into a log, and chill before serving.

MAKES ½ CUP

Prep: **5 minutes** | Fermentation: **24 hours** | Chilling: **1 to 2 hours** | Storage: **1 week**

Note:

DIY HACK: *To make cultured butter by hand, pour the cultured cream into a quart jar and seal tightly with a lid. Shake the cream vigorously until butter begins to clump, then slow down the shaking so that the butter comes together. This is a fun way to get kids involved in the kitchen—let them race to see who can make butter first.*

CHAPTER SEVEN

Grains and Breads

Fermenting grains increases their digestibility and gives them a serious boost in flavor. As with the other types of fermentation, fermentation of grains was developed to serve a specific purpose. In the case of sourdough, fermentation provides natural leavening and its characteristic infusion of sourness, while the fermentation of other cereal grains helps ease digestion and speed up cooking times. Today you can easily incorporate these simple methods into your kitchen routine, and open your taste buds to sweet and savory fermented porridges, as well as a medley of sourdough breads, rolls, and muffins.

Recipes

GRAIN FERMENTATION BASICS

If you have ever wondered why sourdough tastes the way it does, it is due to fermentation. Though it's a simple process, the fermentation of grains has largely fallen by the wayside in modern American society. However, this type of preparation can be particularly helpful to those sensitive to gluten and other grains.

Getting Prepared

• **Plan ahead.** If you plan on fermenting grains for your next meal, you may be too late! This process takes some time, so ease into it. Getting a sourdough starter going will take about a week, while some other processes can be completed in a couple days. Either way, the hands-on time is minimal, but be sure to plan accordingly so your grains have plenty of time to catch up with your ultimate goals for them.

• **Ratios are key.** There is no place in this book where ratios are more important than in baking. Baked goods are notoriously unforgiving, so be sure to follow the recipes exactly and measure your ingredients the right way, with level cups and measuring spoons. It's especially important not to pack flour into cups, but rather to spoon it in gently and then scrape the excess off the top with a knife.

The Fermentation Process

• **Regular feeding wins the race.** For a sourdough starter and other grains you want to ferment, the best way to have continual success is to feed the grains regularly. While you can take breaks now and again (as outlined in subsequent pages), especially at the beginning it's important to feed your starters consistently to allow them to flourish.

• **Fermentation is different for everyone.** The temperature, yeast, and bacteria present in your kitchen have a significant effect on the outcome of your ferments. By following these recipes, but also adjusting certain factors based on your individual needs, you can turn out great ferments. If your starter takes longer than suggested, don't worry. Adjust the plan to work with your individual starter. As you go along, take notes and pay close attention to your ferments so you begin to know what to expect.

SOURDOUGH STARTER
TROUBLESHOOTING TIPS

The most common problem with sourdough is that the starter does not rise. If this is the case with your starter, chances are it just needs more time. While 24 hours is typically enough time, a cooler fermenting space can stall things a bit, too. When in doubt, try giving it 12 more hours and see how things look then.

Is it bubbling? Bubbling is a sure sign that fermentation is taking place. If it is bubbling, even slightly, this is a good sign and shows that things are moving in the right direction. Chances are it just needs more time to get fermentation fully underway.

Did you switch flours? Switching flours can be difficult on a starter, requiring an adjustment period. Continue to feed your starter regularly with the new flour until the starter is doubling between feedings again.

When in doubt, feed it. If you are concerned that your starter is not working, and you have waited at least 48 hours, try feeding it again with ½ cup flour and ¼ cup water to see if that gets things going.

Mold growth. Mold can grow on a sourdough starter more easily than on many other ferments. The most important thing to remember is to scrape down the sides of the fermentation vessel, as any flour particles left on the sides are prone to mold growth. If mold occurs, throw the starter out and begin again another day.

SOURDOUGH STARTER

MAKES 1 STARTER   Prep: **15 minutes** | Fermentation: **6 days** | Storage: **2 to 3 weeks**

People I talk to are often daunted by the process of making sourdough. While I am the first to admit that creating a good sourdough starter takes some time and love, the process itself, like many other processes in this book, is rather easy. If you enjoy the tangy taste of a good sourdough bread, this is a great tool to allow you to make your own at home. Once you get a starter going, you can keep it healthy and alive for years if you take care of it. Using bacteria and yeasts in the air around you, each sourdough starter is unique to its own environment.

2½ cups whole-wheat flour
1½ cups water, divided
½ cup all-purpose flour

1   In a quart jar, combine ½ cup of the whole-wheat flour and ¼ cup of the water. Stir and scrape down the sides of the jar. Cover the jar with a clean kitchen towel and place it for 24 hours in a location that maintains a temperature between 65° and 85°F.

2   Once the starter becomes active (it will be bubbling and rising), feed it again by adding an additional ½ cup whole-wheat flour and ¼ cup water. Stir well, replace the kitchen towel, and leave it for another 24 hours.

continues ►

Grains and Breads

3   Discard half of the starter, and feed it again with another ½ cup whole-wheat flour and ¼ cup water. Stir well, replace the towel, and leave it for an additional 24 hours.

4   Repeat step 3 two more times, discarding half of the starter each time and feeding it again. During this time, the starter should reliably begin to double in size between feedings. When this is achieved, discard half of the starter and feed it one final time, this time using ½ cup all-purpose flour and the last ¼ cup water. Let it sit for a final 24 hours before using.

Notes:

A CLOSER LOOK: *In between batches, simply refrigerate your starter culture in a covered container. When you are ready to use it again, discard half of the culture and feed the remainder for 3 days at room temperature as instructed above, and it will be ready to go again.*

SOURDOUGH PANCAKES

Made with only sourdough starter and no additional flour, these fluffy, flavorful pancakes are heavenly. Top them with Crème Fraîche (page 141) or with fermented fruit syrups such as Lacto-Fermented Raspberry-Mint Syrup (page 99) or Fermented Blackberry-Sage Syrup (page 100). You will need 2 cups of starter for this recipe, and the starter must be at room temperature. If your starter is refrigerated, take it out the night before and feed it so that you have plenty. And be sure to reserve a bit to keep your starter going.

2 cups Sourdough Starter (page 149)

1 large egg, beaten

¼ cup unsalted butter, melted

1 tablespoon sugar

½ teaspoon sea salt

1 teaspoon baking soda

1 tablespoon water

Vegetable oil, for frying

1 In a large bowl, combine the sourdough starter, egg, butter, sugar, and salt. Mix well to combine.

2 In a small bowl, stir the baking soda into the water. Set aside.

3 Heat a griddle or frying pan over medium-high heat and add a small amount of oil. Right before you begin cooking, stir the baking soda–water mixture into the dough.

4 Ladle about ¼ cup pancake batter into the pan for each pancake and cook until they are golden brown, about 2 minutes on each side. Remove from the heat and serve.

MAKES ABOUT 10 PANCAKES   Prep: **5 minutes** | Cook: **4 minutes** | Storage: **5 days**

Notes:

SEASONAL SWAP: *I absolutely love pancakes with fruit in them, though not everyone in my family enjoys them as much as I do. Try dressing these up by adding a cup of your favorite berries or whatever seasonal fruit you prefer to the batter for a fruity and delicious breakfast.*

WHOLE-GRAIN SOURDOUGH LOAF

This loaf requires a few hours of preparation time, but it is well worth the wait. In fact, you'll get the best flavor and rise if you chill the loaf overnight and let it rise again the next day. Bounding with tangy flavor, this loaf is great for slicing. Serve it with a bowl of hearty soup in the winter, or pair it with a loaded dinner salad in warmer months.

1¼ cups Sourdough Starter
  (page 149)
1 cup water
1 tablespoon unsalted butter,
  at room temperature
1 tablespoon raw honey
1¼ teaspoons sea salt
4 cups whole-wheat flour

1 In a large bowl, mix the starter and water. Add the butter, honey, and salt. Finally, add the flour, and mix until all is well combined. Knead the dough for 8 to 10 minutes, until it is smooth.

2 Lightly grease a bowl and transfer the dough to the bowl. Cover loosely with a piece of plastic wrap. Leave the dough at room temperature until it has doubled in size, 2 to 3 hours.

3 Lightly grease a Dutch oven. Gently punch the dough down and transfer it to the Dutch oven. Cover the loaf with a piece of lightly greased plastic wrap and refrigerate it overnight.

4 The following day, remove the Dutch oven from the refrigerator and let the dough come to room temperature and rise, 3 to 4 hours total.

5 Preheat the oven to 350°F.

6 Bake the bread in the Dutch oven, uncovered, until the top is well browned, about 55 minutes.

MAKES 1 LOAF

Prep: **20 minutes** | Rise: **5 to 7 hours, plus overnight** | Bake: **55 minutes** | Storage: **3 to 5 days**

Notes:

SOURDOUGH DINNER ROLLS

If you envision a crusty soured loaf when you hear the words "sourdough bread," think again! Soft and airy, these buttery rolls work well with salad, soup, or, well, pretty much any meal that requires a little something extra. The sourdough starter provides a little lift but is backed up by the instant yeast in this recipe to create a super fluffy roll.

3 cups all-purpose flour

½ cup Sourdough Starter
  (page 149)

⅔ cup lukewarm water

5 tablespoons unsalted butter,
  at room temperature

1 large egg, beaten

1 tablespoon sugar

1½ teaspoons instant yeast

1 teaspoon sea salt

1 Combine all the ingredients in a large bowl and mix together well. Knead until a soft, smooth dough is formed.

2 Lightly grease a smaller bowl and transfer the dough to that bowl. Cover loosely with a piece of plastic wrap. Let the dough sit at room temperature until it has doubled in size, 1½ to 2 hours.

3 Grease 2 (9-inch) cake pans.

4 Gently punch the dough down and transfer it to a lightly greased surface. Roll the dough into a log about 3 inches in diameter. Cut the dough into 16 equal portions by first cutting the dough in half, and then cutting each portion in half and then in quarters.

5 Roll each piece of dough into a ball and place 8 balls in each cake pan, evenly spaced apart. Cover loosely with plastic wrap and let rise at room temperature until the rolls have become puffy, about 1 hour.

6 Toward the end of rising, preheat the oven to 350°F.

7 Bake the rolls until golden brown, 22 to 25 minutes.

MAKES ABOUT 16 ROLLS

Prep: **20 minutes** | Rise: **2½ to 3 hours** | Bake: **22 to 25 minutes** | Storage: **1 week**

Notes:

SOURDOUGH BAGUETTES

Making sourdough baguettes is not for the impatient, but it's no trouble to those who appreciate a good baguette. These baguettes have a crusty brown exterior and a light, airy interior. They work wonderfully for bánh mì, even though they are not exactly traditional. The sourdough flavor is present but not overpowering, and yeast helps the breads rise well—which won't even be an issue if you feed your starter before using.

BREAD:

1 cup Sourdough Starter (page 149)

2½ cups all-purpose flour, plus more if necessary

¾ cup lukewarm water

1¼ teaspoons sea salt

1 teaspoon sugar

1½ teaspoons instant yeast

GLAZE:

1 large egg yolk

1 tablespoon cold water

1 In a large bowl, mix all the bread ingredients. As the dough forms into a ball, begin to knead it. The dough should be a bit sticky as you begin, but you can add a little extra flour if necessary. Knead by hand or in a stand mixer for 8 to 10 minutes.

2 Transfer the dough to a smaller, lightly greased bowl. Cover the bowl with a clean kitchen towel and let it sit at room temperature until it doubles in size, about 1½ hours.

3 Lightly grease a large baking sheet. Gently press the dough down and divide it into three pieces. Working with one piece at a time, shape the dough into a log about 15 inches long. Press the dough log flat and fold the piece lengthwise, pressing the edges together. Again, flatten the dough log and fold it lengthwise, pressing the seam together. Place the baguette-shaped dough on the baking sheet with the seam side down. Repeat with the remaining two loaves and place them on the baking sheet, making sure they're not touching. Cover the loaves loosely with a piece of lightly greased plastic wrap and let them rise at room temperature until they are puffy, 1 to 2 hours.

4 Meanwhile, preheat the oven to 450°F.

5 Whisk together the egg yolk and water for the glaze. Once the loaves are well risen, brush them with this mixture.

6 Bake the baguettes until well browned, about 25 minutes. Let the baguettes rest in the oven until cool.

MAKES 3 BAGUETTES

Prep: **20 minutes** | Rise: **2½ to 3½ hours** | Bake: **25 minutes** | Storage: **3 days**

Notes:

BLUEBERRY SOURDOUGH MUFFINS

This recipe creates beautifully fluffed muffins that beam with fresh blueberry flavor. Serve them for breakfast or an afternoon snack with tea. Use freshly fed sourdough starter for best results, although if all you have is unfed starter, that will work. Baking soda helps provide some rising action, but the muffins won't be airy without the freshly fed sourdough.

1 cup Sourdough Starter (page 149)

1 cup whole-wheat flour

½ cup raw honey

¼ cup unsalted butter, melted

1 large egg, beaten

1 teaspoon pure vanilla extract

¼ teaspoon sea salt

1 teaspoon baking soda

½ cup blueberries, fresh or frozen

1 Mix the sourdough starter and flour in a large bowl. Cover with plastic wrap and leave at room temperature for 4 hours.

2 Preheat the oven to 400°F. Grease the cups of a standard muffin tin, or insert paper liners into the cups.

3 In a small bowl, combine the honey, butter, egg, vanilla, and salt and mix well. Add this mixture to the flour-starter mixture and stir well to combine. Sprinkle the baking soda over the mixture, then stir briefly to incorporate. Fold in the blueberries. Scoop about ¼ cup batter into each muffin cup.

4 Bake until the tops are golden brown, about 20 minutes.

MAKES 12 MUFFINS Prep: **20 minutes** | Rise: **4 hours** | Bake: **20 minutes** | Storage: **5 days**

Notes:

SEASONAL SWAP: *These muffins can be made with other fruits and berries, based on what is available to you. Apples are great when added fresh to muffins, but other berries like raspberries and cherries can make them really watery. If you'd like to try more options, go for dried fruits such as golden raisins, dried cranberries, or dried cherries.*

SOURDOUGH PIZZA DOUGH

Sourdough pizza dough is airy and delicious, and it lacks the tang of a typical sourdough bread. Rich in flavor, this dough can be topped with anything your heart desires. It's a great use for the extra sourdough starter you toss out at feeding time.

1 cup Sourdough Starter
  (page 149)
½ cup lukewarm water
2½ cups all-purpose flour
1 teaspoon sea salt
½ teaspoon instant yeast

1 Mix all the ingredients together in a large bowl and knead for about 10 minutes. Lightly grease a smaller bowl and transfer the dough to that bowl. Cover the bowl with a piece of lightly greased plastic wrap. Let the dough rise at room temperature until it is doubled in size, 2 to 4 hours.

2 Generously grease a sheet pan. Shape the dough into a large oval and place it in the pan. Cover the dough again with the greased plastic wrap, and let rise again for about 1 hour.

3 Preheat the oven to 450°F.

4 Bake the crust for 8 minutes. Remove it from the oven, add your desired toppings, and bake for an additional 10 minutes.

MAKES 1 CRUST

Prep: **20 minutes** | Rise: **3 to 5 hours** | Bake: **18 minutes** | Storage: **3 to 5 days**

Notes:

OGI

In the West, sweetened breakfasts are a mainstay, but in many places around the world, savory breakfasts are just as common. This simple porridge, popular in Nigeria, Kenya, and Ethiopia, is made from millet, an underutilized grain in America. It is served in many different styles throughout the region and can be prepared in either sweet or savory applications.

2 cups millet
5 cups water, divided
1 teaspoon sea salt

1 In a blender or food processor, coarsely grind the millet. Transfer it to a large jar and add 4 cups of the water and the salt. Cover with a clean kitchen towel and let sit at room temperature for 48 hours.

2 Remove 2 cups of the fermented millet, leaving behind at least 1 cup starter, and transfer it to a small saucepan. Add the remaining 1 cup water and simmer over medium heat until a porridge consistency is achieved, 5 to 10 minutes.

3 Add more millet and water to the starter as desired, cover, and continue to ferment the millet for another 48 hours.

MAKES 4 SERVINGS, PLUS STARTER

Prep: **5 minutes** | Fermentation: **48 hours** | Cook: **5 to 10 minutes** | Storage: **3 days**

Notes:

A CLOSER LOOK: *Millet can be seasoned in the same way as oatmeal, adding the usual cohorts of butter, milk, maple syrup, or jam. Or, if you prefer, you can opt for savory flavorings and add chiles, scallions, and ginger for a cleansing meal. Alternatively, try spices such as coriander, ginger, and turmeric along with coconut milk for a savory-sweet combination.*

FERMENTED STEEL-CUT OAT PORRIDGE

When I was a kid, I hated oatmeal, preferring dry cereal any day. So I consider it a great feat of parenting that my children love the stuff. They have been eating this soured steel-cut oatmeal for years, and actually refuse to eat the old-fashioned oats of my childhood. This simple ferment is easy to get going, and once it is started, you can feed the starter in the same way you do a sourdough starter (see page 149) to keep it going in perpetuity.

2 cups steel-cut oats
2 cups water
2 tablespoons whey (page 31)
½ teaspoon sea salt

1 In a large jar, combine the oats, water, and whey. Cover with a clean kitchen towel and let sit at room temperature for 48 hours. The grains will expand during this time.

2 Remove nearly 2 cups of the mixture, leaving behind at least 1 cup of starter, and transfer it to a small saucepan. Cover with water and cook over medium heat until the oats are tender, about 15 minutes. Add more water, if desired, to thin the oatmeal.

3 Add more oats and water to the starter as desired, cover, and continue to ferment the oatmeal for another 48 hours.

MAKES 4 SERVINGS, PLUS STARTER

Prep: **5 minutes** | Fermentation: **48 hours** | Cook: **15 minutes** | Storage: **3 days**

Notes:

A CLOSER LOOK: *My favorite way to flavor oatmeal is to add 1 to 2 teaspoons of ground cinnamon, 1 tablespoon butter, and 1 tablespoon pure maple syrup to the pot toward the end of cooking. The cinnamon offsets the soured flavor of the oatmeal and allows you to use less sweetener. Top the oatmeal with dried cherries, raisins, cranberries, walnuts, pecans, or hazelnuts for a filling meal.*

RAGI

Ragi is the Southern Indian version of ogi. This alternative breakfast cereal is also gluten-free, making it a perfect option for someone on a gluten-free diet. Because it is a whole grain, a little goes a long way, making this a filling breakfast that requires little effort.

5 cups water, divided
2 cups millet
1 teaspoon sea salt
1 teaspoon vegetable oil
½ teaspoon mustard seeds
½ teaspoon coriander seeds
2 tablespoons Yogurt (page 134)

1 In a large jar, combine 4 cups of the water, the millet, and the salt. Cover with a clean kitchen towel and let sit at room temperature for 48 hours.

2 Remove nearly 2 cups of the mixture, leaving behind at least 1 cup of starter, and transfer it to a blender. Process until a thick paste forms as the millet is ground. Transfer to a saucepan and add the remaining 1 cup water. Bring to a boil over medium-high heat, then reduce the heat and simmer until a thick consistency is achieved, 5 to 10 minutes.

3 In a small skillet, heat the oil over medium-high heat. Add the mustard and coriander seeds and heat until they begin to sizzle and pop. Once this occurs, quickly transfer the seeds to the ragi. Add the yogurt, stir well, and serve.

4 Add more millet and water to the starter as desired, cover, and continue to ferment the millet for another 48 hours.

MAKES 4 SERVINGS, PLUS STARTER

Prep: **5 minutes** | Fermentation: **48 hours** | Cook: **5 to 10 minutes** | Storage: **3 days**

Notes:

A CLOSER LOOK: *This type of porridge can also be made sweet by adding a little brown sugar and the crushed seeds from 1 or 2 cardamom pods. Top the porridge with your favorite chopped nuts for a complete and filling meal.*

SOURDOUGH BISCUITS

Biscuits are a favorite in my house, and I hope they become one in yours as well. Making them from scratch requires only a few minutes of active time, and pairing them with home-made jam makes them an exquisite start to the day. Use sourdough starter that would be tossed out for this recipe to help keep your starter in check, and enjoy the tangy flavor of sourdough in this simple and quick project. A pastry blender makes the prep work easier, but you can also use two knives to create the same effect.

2 cups all-purpose flour
½ teaspoon salt
1 teaspoon baking powder
1 teaspoon baking soda
1 tablespoon sugar
6 tablespoons cold butter, plus melted butter for brushing (optional)
1¼ cup sourdough starter

1 Preheat the oven to 400°F.

2 In a large bowl, combine the flour, salt, baking powder, baking soda, and sugar. Mix well.

3 Cut the butter into small pieces and add it to the flour mixture. Using a pastry blender, cut the butter into the flour until the butter is in small granules. This does not require perfection, but try to break up the bigger pieces so there are not clumps of butter.

4 Make a small hole in the middle of the flour mixture. Pour the sourdough starter into the hole, and use a fork to mix the starter with the flour. The biscuit dough will be dry, but will hold together. Once mixed, knead it a few times in the bowl using clean, dry hands.

5 Using your hands, shape the dough into 10 small, rounded biscuits. Place the biscuits on the baking sheet, pressing them down slightly as you place them on the sheet. Cook them for 15 minutes, until the tops are golden brown. Brush the biscuits with butter when complete, if using.

MAKES 10 BISCUITS   Prep: **10 minutes** | Cook: **15 minutes** | Storage: **3 days**

Notes:

CHAPTER EIGHT

Condiments and Vinegars

In case you haven't gotten the picture by this point, this chapter will drive the message home: pretty much everything under the sun can be fermented. Yes, all your favorite smears, spreads, dips, and sauces can be made tastier and healthier through the art-science-work of fermentation. Probably some of the simplest introductions to ferments for newcomers, condiments and vinegars make tasty additions to many meals. In this chapter, you'll find recipes for several different vinegars, as well as favorite condiments like ketchup, mayonnaise, mustard, and more.

Recipes

FERMENTING CONDIMENTS AND VINEGARS

These are some of the easiest ferments in the book, as most require little work beyond the initial mixing stage. In the end, you can create a product far tastier than store-bought varieties, and teeming with beneficial probiotics to nourish your body.

Getting Started

* **Vinegars require minimal work.** Basically, you set them aside, and they do the work for you. It's that easy, which is why they are probably one of the easiest ferments for you to begin immediately. They require more time than many other ferments to complete, but in terms of getting started, they are just right for right now.

* **Condiments are all similar to fruit ferments.** With the exception of some chutneys, they all contain starter cultures and will ferment readily on their own. You will not see active fermentation as with vegetable ferments, so don't wait for it to happen. Follow the directions and your condiments will be well fermented and ready for use.

The Fermentation Process

* **To make vinegar, you need alcohol.** This is why the process takes so long. The sugars must first convert to alcohol, which then converts to vinegar. Do not be concerned if your fruit mixture begins to take on an alcoholic aroma, as that is exactly what it should be doing, and a sign you are headed in the right direction.

* **Keep it covered.** Both vinegars and condiments are irresistible to fruit flies and other bugs. For this reason, be sure to keep things covered during fermentation to prevent contamination. For vinegars that call for a kitchen towel to cover the ferment, be sure to secure it using a rubber band. Vinegar requires oxygen for fermentation. Once it's done, store your vinegar in an airtight bottle to halt fermentation. Vinegar does not need to be refrigerated.

* **Follow times indicated.** Because you won't see any visual proof of fermentation for these projects, you may be tempted to leave them out on the counter longer than indicated. Please don't. While a couple of hours either way is not going to hurt you, an extra day or two could spoil your food. Err on the side of caution, and follow the timelines provided to prevent spoilage.

VINEGARS
TROUBLESHOOTING TIPS

Vinegars are one of the simplest ferments to get right; however, that does not mean you will never run into problems. Here are some basic troubleshooting tips to keep your vinegars on track.

Scum on surface. As with vegetable and fruit ferments, long fermentation times can lead to scum forming on the surface of the juice or vinegar. Keep a watchful eye during fermentation, and skim off the scum as it appears on a daily basis. Failure to skim the scum regularly can result in mold growth. If this happens, skim off the mold and scum and continue, skimming more frequently going forward.

Fruit flies in vinegar. Fruit flies can be very pesky around fermenting juice and wine. To prevent them from getting in, always keep the vinegar covered with a clean kitchen towel secured by a rubber band. Avoid the use of cheesecloth and other porous materials, which can allow fruit flies access to the ferment. Be sure to keep the container covered when you are tasting or doing any other work on the vinegar as well.

Disappearing juice. Depending on the time of year and your climate, you may notice that the level of your juice or vinegar decreases during fermentation. Evaporation occurs as a result of longer fermenting times and is completely normal.

Nothing is happening. Like many other ferments, you won't be able to see much going on in a vinegar ferment while the process is taking place, especially after the conversion to alcohol. For this reason, be sure to follow the times listed, and begin tasting the vinegar early to gauge how it is developing. Once it tastes like vinegar, it is finished and ready for bottling.

APPLE CIDER VINEGAR

MAKES ABOUT 3 CUPS   Prep: **15 minutes** | Fermentation: **1 to 2 months** | Storage: **1 year**

Raw apple cider vinegar is a formidable health tonic, as well as a great multipurpose seasoning in your kitchen. Save the scraps from several apples and get going on a batch today. It is so simple, you can place it off to the side and virtually forget about it—after a couple of months, you will have vinegar. Make this from fall apples, which are the sweetest, and preferably when you are baking a pie or another large project that yields lots of discarded skins and cores.

2 cups apple scraps (skins, cores)
3½ cups water
¼ cup raw honey

1   In a quart jar, combine the apple scraps, water, and honey. Give the mixture a good stir.

2   Cover the jar with a clean kitchen cloth secured by a rubber band. Leave the jar at room temperature and swirl it around once or twice a day to agitate and aerate the contents.

continues ▶

3   In a little over a week, the apple scraps will sink to the bottom, and the mixture will have become alcoholic. When this occurs, strain the solids from the liquid and discard them.

4   Pour the liquid into a clean jar and cover with a clean kitchen towel secured by a rubber band. Leave at room temperature, again gently swirling the jar daily to aerate the liquid.

Somewhere between 1 to 2 months, depending on a variety of factors, the cider will change to vinegar. Begin tasting it at 1 month—when it tastes like vinegar, it's done. Bottle it in swing-top bottles for storage.

Notes:

A CLOSER LOOK: *Apple cider vinegar is great for cooking, but don't use it for canning. Vinegar that is used for canning must be 5 percent acidity. Using test strips that measure pH, you can get a good picture of how acidic your vinegar is, but unless you can get it tested in a lab, it should be devoted exclusively to fresh uses in your kitchen.*

PLUM VINEGAR

Plums come in many sizes and colors. Some are smaller than a golf ball, while others are nearly the size of a peach. They can be purple, red, yellow, and every shade in between. Just about any type will work for this vinegar, although the darker the skin, the more colorful your end product will be. Unlike the underripe whole plums fermented in chapter 5, these plums should be fully ripened to make this sweet, complex vinegar.

3 ripe plums
3 cups water
¼ cup raw honey

1 Roughly chop the plums, discarding the pits, and put them in a quart jar. Add the water and honey, and give it all a good stir.

2 Cover the jar with a clean kitchen towel secured by a rubber band. After 1 week, strain out the fruit, return the liquid to the jar, and cover it again with a towel secured by a rubber band. Leave the jar at room temperature for 7 more weeks. Stir it about once per week to aerate it. When the vinegar is complete, strain it through a fine-mesh strainer and store it in a swing-top bottle.

MAKES 1 QUART   Prep: **15 minutes** | Fermentation: **2 months** | Storage: **1 year**

Notes:

A CLOSER LOOK: *Plum vinegar is a great condiment for dressing a salad, but it can also be reduced further to use as a glaze on meats and poultry. To do this, simmer the vinegar for 10 to 15 minutes until reduced by half.*

BLACKBERRY KOMBUCHA VINEGAR

In the Pacific Northwest, blackberries are hiding around every turn come August. While they can quickly take over your yard if left unchecked, as an unexpected treat along the road, they are nothing short of incredible. If you want to capture the taste of summer in a bottle of vinegar, make this ferment while blackberries are ripe and easily accessible. This recipe uses a SCOBY, so if you have an old one sitting around or even a small piece of a current one, now is a good time to use it.

2 cups blackberries

3 cups water

¼ cup raw honey

1 SCOBY (page 191)

1 In a small bowl, lightly crush the berries until they begin to release their juices. Pour the berries and juice into a quart jar. Add the water and honey and give it all a good stir.

2 Place the SCOBY in the jar, gently easing it in if it is larger than the mouth of the jar. Cover the jar with a clean kitchen towel secured by a rubber band. Leave the jar at room temperature for 2 months. When the vinegar is complete, strain it through a fine-mesh strainer into a swing-top bottle.

MAKES 1 QUART   Prep: **15 minutes** | Fermentation: **2 months** | Storage: **1 year**

Notes:

SEASONAL SWAP: *Use blackberry vinegar in place of balsamic vinegar in the kitchen. Its sweet flavor is similar, and it goes well with a variety of produce in salads and sauces. It can provide fruity flavor to a strictly vegetable green salad or one topped with other seasonal berries, and it generally rounds out a meal based on late-summer ingredients.*

RED WINE VINEGAR

Red wine comes at a premium, which is why tossing a half-empty bottle that is past its prime can be hard. You'll never have to face that dilemma again when you make your own red wine vinegar. This recipe is specifically designed for some leftover wine that would otherwise be tossed. If you want to make more, simply multiply the recipe.

1 cup red wine

3 tablespoons raw apple cider vinegar

1 In a small bowl or jar, combine the red wine and apple cider vinegar. Stir well and cover with a clean kitchen towel. Stir regularly, at least once every few days, to aerate the wine.

2 Taste the wine vinegar after about 1 month. If it is soured to your liking, it is done. If not, ferment it for up to 1 additional week. Store in a swing-top bottle.

MAKES 1 CUP   Prep: **5 minutes** | Fermentation: **4 to 5 weeks** | Storage: **1 year**

Notes:

FERMENTED MUSTARD

This type of mustard makes use of a common item that may otherwise get thrown away in the home of a fermenting family: pickle brine. Simple and sweet, this stress-free process lets you get your probiotics even when you are simply smearing a sandwich with the most familiar of condiments.

¾ cup fermented pickle brine

½ cup brown or yellow
   mustard seeds

1 tablespoon chopped shallot

1 tablespoon raw honey

1 Combine the pickle brine, mustard seeds, shallot, and honey in a bowl. Cover with a clean kitchen cloth and let sit at room temperature for 12 hours.

2 Use a countertop blender, food processor, or immersion blender to purée the mustard. For a chunky mustard, blend lightly; for a smooth mustard, purée for up to 2 minutes. Transfer to a jar, cover, and refrigerate.

MAKES 1 CUP Prep: **10 minutes** | Fermentation: **12 hours** | Storage: **3 to 4 months**

Notes:

MAKE IT A MEAL: *Whole-grain mustards have a similar flavor to blended mustard, but their unique look has a lot more character. I like to use whole-grain mustard in broccoli-cheddar soup. To make it, dice an onion and a large potato and sauté them in oil until the onion becomes translucent. Add the florets from a head or two of broccoli, and cover with chicken or vegetable stock or water. Simmer for several minutes, until the broccoli is tender. Purée the soup with an immersion blender, add about 1 tablespoon whole-grain mustard and a couple handfuls of shredded cheddar cheese, and you have dinner.*

FERMENTED KETCHUP

Ketchup is a condiment that has become so synonymous with the grocery store that few people know how to make it at home anymore. The benefit of making it yourself, however, is that you have better control over the ingredients, especially sugar, which is quite heavily added to commercial varieties. Instead of sweetening with high-fructose corn syrup, this version uses honey to add that familiar sweetness to this staple condiment.

1½ cups tomato paste

3 tablespoons raw honey

2 tablespoons whey (page 31) or
    sauerkraut brine (page 41)

2 garlic cloves, peeled and
    smashed with the back of a knife

1½ teaspoons pickling salt

½ teaspoon ground cloves

½ teaspoon ground allspice

1 In a pint jar, mix all the ingredients well. Cover the jar with a lid and leave it at room temperature.

2 Begin tasting the ketchup after 48 hours; when the flavor is to your liking, transfer it to the refrigerator to halt fermentation.

MAKES 2 CUPS Prep: **5 minutes** | Fermentation: **48 to 72 hours** | Storage: **3 to 4 months**

Notes:

A CLOSER LOOK: *If you want more sweetness in this recipe, feel free to add more honey to taste. It is surprising how much sugar is in commercial ketchup and how our palates have become accustomed to equating this traditional condiment with a strong underlying sweetness.*

FERMENTED BARBECUE SAUCE

You may not realize it, but making condiments yourself can be a breeze. While it's certainly simpler to just buy them, for about 10 minutes of your time, you can avoid all those unnecessary preservatives and additives—and save money along the way. This barbecue sauce works equally well for dipping and slathering.

1¼ cups tomato paste

¼ cup pure maple syrup

2 tablespoons raw apple
   cider vinegar

1 tablespoon raw honey

1 teaspoon sea salt

½ teaspoon chili powder

¼ teaspoon cayenne pepper

⅛ teaspoon garlic powder

⅛ teaspoon onion powder

⅛ teaspoon ground allspice

⅛ teaspoon ground cloves

2 tablespoons whey (page 31)

1 In a pint jar, combine the tomato paste, maple syrup, apple cider vinegar, honey, and all the spices. Mix well. Add the whey and stir briefly to combine.

2 Cover the jar with a lid and let it sit at room temperature for 2 days. Transfer to the refrigerator.

MAKES 2 CUPS   Prep: **10 minutes** | Fermentation: **2 days** | Storage: **1 month**

Notes:

A CLOSER LOOK: *If you are using this on the grill with meat or poultry, keep in mind that the high temperatures kill the healthy bacteria in the sauce. To get around this, add some to the meat when grilling, and then give a final dip in the sauce after food is off the grill, if desired.*

FERMENTED MAYO

Mayonnaise gets a bad rap for being difficult to prepare, but in truth, if you are willing to do the whisking, you can produce an amazingly delicious mayo quite easily. If you prefer not to whisk, you can always use a food processor or immersion blender to get the job done. Make sure all your ingredients are at room temperature before beginning, or this will not emulsify as desired. The trick is to pour the oil slowly, even stopping at times, if necessary, between blending, to ensure that it becomes fully emulsified.

2 large egg yolks

1½ tablespoons raw apple cider vinegar

1 cup grapeseed oil

1 tablespoon whey (page 31)

1 teaspoon Dijon mustard

½ teaspoon sea salt

1 In a small bowl, whisk together the egg yolks and apple cider vinegar.

2 Slowly add the oil, one drop at a time, to the bowl. Whisk thoroughly after each drop to ensure that the egg yolk emulsifies with the oil. Continue to slowly add the oil until it is all thoroughly blended in. As you get further through the oil, you can slightly speed up pouring the oil into the yolk mixture, from a drop to a thin stream, but be sure to stop frequently to ensure that the oil is emulsifying.

3 Whisk the whey, mustard, and salt into the mayonnaise. Affix a cap and leave the mayonnaise at room temperature for 7 hours. Transfer to the refrigerator.

MAKES 1¼ CUPS   Prep: **15 minutes** | Fermentation: **7 hours** | Storage: **2 weeks**

Notes:

A CLOSER LOOK: *Use this mayonnaise as a jumping off point for many other sauces. Mix it with garlic to make a delicious dipping sauce, or add roasted red peppers or sun-dried tomatoes for a fabulous sandwich spread.*

CREAMY KEFIR SALAD DRESSING

In this recipe, kefir is strained to produce a thicker texture. I also like doing a 10- to 12-hour secondary ferment to really infuse the garlicky flavor, but you can omit that step if you are in a rush. Don't skip the straining step, though, as that creates the thick consistency everyone loves in a ranch-style dressing.

2 cups Kefir (page 125)

4 garlic cloves, peeled

1 tablespoon freshly squeezed lemon juice

2 teaspoons dried parsley

1 teaspoon sea salt

½ teaspoon freshly ground black pepper

1 Line a mesh strainer with a coffee filter and set the strainer over a bowl. Put the kefir in the strainer and let it drain for 20 minutes.

2 In a pint jar, combine the drained kefir and the garlic cloves. Cover the jar and leave it at room temperature for 12 hours.

3 Remove the garlic cloves, wipe them off, and mince them, then return them to the jar. Mix in the lemon juice, parsley, salt, and pepper, cover, and refrigerate for at least 30 minutes before serving.

MAKES 2 CUPS   Prep: **30 minutes** | Fermentation: **12 hours** | Storage: **2 weeks**

Notes:

DIY HACK: *If you don't want to spend the cash on new mason jars, you can simply repurpose old glass jars for these projects. Unlike in canning, where jars should not be reused, in fermentation this poses no problem, as you are not heat-processing the finished ferment. Save glass mayonnaise, spaghetti sauce, or other food storage jars to reuse for these recipes.*

LACTO-FERMENTED TOMATO CHUTNEY

Tomato chutney is great on crackers or bread, or even served with rice. Spoon this simple yet complex mixture over just about anything. I like to use plum tomatoes, which have a lower water content and thinner skins that do not need to be removed. If you are tempted to eat this by the spoonful, no one will blame you—just be sure to use a clean spoon.

1 small apple, cored and
   roughly diced
¼ cup lightly packed mint leaves
2 scallions, sliced
3 garlic cloves, peeled
1 (1-inch) piece ginger, peeled
   and roughly chopped
1 jalapeño, halved and seeded
¼ cup raw apple cider vinegar
1 tablespoon cumin seeds
1 teaspoon pickling salt
3 or 4 plum tomatoes, roughly diced
2 tablespoons whey (page 31)

1 In a food processor, combine the apple, mint, scallions, garlic, ginger, jalapeño, apple cider vinegar, cumin seeds, and salt. Process briefly, leaving the chutney still lightly chunky. Stir in the diced tomatoes, and then transfer the mixture to a clean pint jar.

2 Add the whey to the jar and stir briefly to combine. Cover the jar with a lid and leave at room temperature for 2 to 3 days. Transfer to the refrigerator to halt fermentation.

MAKES 2 CUPS Prep: **10 minutes** | Fermentation: **2 to 3 days** | Storage: **1 to 2 months**

Notes:

A CLOSER LOOK: *If you prefer the flavor of heirloom or other tomatoes, you can use those instead, but you must remove their skins. To do this, follow the instructions for removing peach skins on page 182. Once the skins are removed, I'd suggest quartering the tomatoes and placing them in a colander to drain some of their liquid and remove the seeds before using in the recipe.*

LACTO-FERMENTED PEACH CHUTNEY

The flavor of peaches holds up wonderfully in chutney, where a variety of spices and seasonings have a tendency to mask fruit flavor. I find this type of chutney really delicious when paired with a tortilla chip, though I'm well aware that is not its intended purpose. For a sweet and spicy combination that truly shines, pair this chutney with pork or poultry.

¼ cup water

2 tablespoons whey (page 31)

Juice and grated zest of 1 lemon

1 tablespoon sugar

1 teaspoon sea salt

1½ cups peeled, diced peaches

¼ cup golden raisins

¼ cup chopped nuts (such as
   walnuts, hazelnuts, or pecans)

½ teaspoon ground cumin

½ teaspoon red pepper flakes

½ teaspoon coriander seeds

1 In a medium-size bowl, combine the water, whey, lemon juice and zest, sugar, and salt. Add the peaches to the bowl and stir to mix. Add the raisins, nuts, and spices. Pack the mixture into a quart jar, pressing it down slightly to remove air bubbles. Make sure the fruit is submerged below the juices.

2 Cover the jar and let it ferment at room temperature for 2 days. Transfer to the refrigerator to halt fermentation.

MAKES 2 CUPS Prep: **15 minutes** | Fermentation: **2 days** | Storage: **2 months**

Notes:

PREP TIP: *To quickly peel peaches, bring a small pot of water to a boil. While the water is heating, prepare an ice bath by filling a second bowl with ice and water. On the bottom of each peach, score an "X" into the fruit with a small knife. When the water comes to a boil, add the peaches and blanch them for about 30 seconds. Transfer the peaches to the ice bath and let them cool. The skins should then slip off easily. If any do not come off, return them to the boiling water and repeat the process.*

LACTO-FERMENTED PLUM CHUTNEY

Plum chutney is a great way to preserve any extra plums you have lying around. If you know someone with a tree, even better. Come harvest season, it is rather hard to keep up with even a modest-size tree's production. Any type of plum can be used in this recipe, but be sure that they are fully ripe and juicy for optimum flavor in the finished product. This chutney ends up both sweet and a bit spicy. If you like heat, add more jalapeños for an even stronger bite.

2 cups chopped ripe plums

1 cup finely chopped red
   bell pepper

¼ cup chopped onion

1 jalapeño, seeded and minced

2 tablespoons chopped fresh
   mint leaves

2 tablespoons chopped fresh
   cilantro leaves

1 teaspoon grated ginger

2 tablespoons freshly squeezed
   lime juice

2 teaspoons raw honey

½ teaspoon pickling salt

1 tablespoon whey (page 31)

1 In a small bowl, toss together the plums, red pepper, onion, jalapeño, mint, cilantro, ginger, lime juice, honey, and pickling salt. Add the whey and stir briefly. Pack the mixture into a clean pint jar, pressing the mixture down to remove air bubbles and release some juices.

2 If needed, top off the jar with a bit of water to cover the chutney. Place a lid on the jar and leave it at room temperature for 2 to 3 days. Transfer to the refrigerator to halt fermentation.

MAKES 2 CUPS Prep: **15 minutes** | Fermentation: **2 to 3 days** | Storage: **2 months**

Notes:

FERMENTED CUCUMBER RELISH

This simple relish is a classic example of how you can introduce probiotics into every meal. Spread it on a hot dog or hamburger to increase the health benefits of your backyard cookout. Simple to make, and rivaling any commercial relish, this condiment is perfect for kids or adults who might otherwise resist eating or even tasting fermented foods.

3 cups diced cucumber

1 green bell pepper,
   seeded and diced

1 red bell pepper,
   seeded and diced

1 small onion, diced

3 garlic cloves, peeled and minced

1 teaspoon dill seed

¾ teaspoon mustard seed

2 tablespoons pickling salt

3 cups water

1 In a small bowl, toss together the cucumber, bell peppers, onion, and garlic. Stir in the dill and mustard seeds. Pack the mixture into a quart jar, pressing down gently to extract some liquids.

2 In a small bowl, dissolve the salt in the water, then pour this brine over the cucumber mixture to cover. Press the relish down with a nonreactive utensil to release any air bubbles.

3 Place a lid on the jar and let it ferment at room temperature for 3 to 4 days. Transfer to the refrigerator to halt fermentation.

MAKES 1 QUART   Prep: **10 minutes** | Fermentation: **3 to 4 days** | Storage: **2 to 3 months**

Notes:

SEASONAL SWAP: *Zucchini can be substituted in this recipe for the cucumbers with no one being the wiser. While this substitution will not work in all cucumber recipes, in this case, where the cucumbers are diced, one is nearly indistinguishable from the other.*

LACTO-FERMENTED TOMATO SALSA

For years, I was the queen of canning tomato salsa, producing enough for my family of four to make it through the winter. However, these days I am more prone to can a smaller quantity and instead make a lot of fermented salsa while tomatoes are fresh. The shelf life is not as long as the canned variety, but I prefer the taste.

4 large tomatoes

1 small onion, diced

1 jalapeño, seeded if desired and minced

3 garlic cloves, peeled and minced

¼ cup chopped fresh cilantro leaves and stems

¼ cup whey (page 31)

2 tablespoons freshly squeezed lime juice

1 teaspoon pickling salt

1 Quarter the tomatoes and remove the seeds. Let them sit in a colander briefly to drain off some of the juices, then dice them.

2 In a small bowl, toss together the diced tomatoes, onion, jalapeño, garlic, cilantro, whey, lime juice, and salt. Pack the salsa into a quart jar, pressing down on the vegetables to release some of the liquid from the tomatoes.

3 Close the jar with a lid and let ferment at room temperature for 2 to 3 days. Transfer to the refrigerator to halt fermentation.

MAKES 1 QUART   Prep: **10 minutes** | Fermentation: **2 to 3 days** | Storage: **1 to 2 months**

Notes:

A CLOSER LOOK: *If you don't want to or aren't able to use whey, there are many other options. You could substitute it with either Kombucha (page 193) or Water Kefir (page 200), or you could simply use 2 teaspoons pickling salt instead of 1 teaspoon.*

FERMENTED CRANBERRY SAUCE

If you are still eating the cranberry sauce extruded from a can come Thanksgiving, it is high time you try out this ferment. Fresh and crisp, this sauce is similar to a chutney in texture; like the stuff from a can, "sauce" isn't quite the right word to describe it. I have never been a big fan of cranberries, but the combination of sweet, sour, and spicy here is a winner even when it's not a holiday.

1 pound cranberries

Grated zest of 1 orange, plus
   2 tablespoons freshly squeezed
   orange juice

1 jalapeño, seeded and minced

1 (2-inch) piece ginger, peeled and
   roughly chopped

¼ cup pure maple syrup

¼ cup whey (page 31)

2 teaspoons pickling salt

1 In a food processor, process all of the ingredients until well combined but still a little chunky. Pack the mixture into a quart jar.

2 Close the jar and let ferment at room temperature. Begin tasting the cranberry sauce after 2 days; when the flavor is to your liking, transfer it to the refrigerator to halt fermentation.

MAKES 1 QUART Prep: **10 minutes** | Fermentation: **2 to 5 days** | Storage: **1 to 2 months**

Notes:

A CLOSER LOOK: *Cranberries are typically available only around their harvest time in the fall. However, they can be frozen for up to 1 year with no reduction in quality. Pick up a couple of bags around the holidays and toss them in the freezer, still sealed, until you are ready to use them. Then simply thaw before making this recipe.*

CHAPTER NINE

Beverages

Fermented beverages are what draw many people to fermentation. Whether it is alcoholic ferments like beer and wine or probiotic ones like kombucha and water kefir, the science is quite similar. You start with a sugary liquid, and through yeast and bacteria, a once-sweet juice is transformed into something wonderfully different, allowing you to create everything from natural sodas to probiotic elixirs and delicious alcoholic brews. In this chapter, you will find an array of fermented beverages, including kombucha, water kefir, shrubs, kvass, and mead.

Recipes

FERMENTING BEVERAGES

The processes are varied and unique, but the science behind them all is the same. Whether you are making an alcoholic drink or a probiotic one, your success is dependent upon one unifying factor: the feeding of yeast and bacteria on sugar.

Getting Prepared

- **Cleanliness is key.** Be sure that you are using clean hands and equipment throughout all stages of fermentation, as the lack of doing so is the most common cause of failure. Clean all equipment well before beginning, and allow to air-dry.

- **Gather equipment and supplies.** Many of the recipes in this chapter require specialty supplies that you probably don't have on hand. Read the recipe well before beginning any project to ensure that you are prepared with the correct cultures and materials. Unless you live in a fermentation-friendly city, you will likely need to mail-order some supplies. You will also need some bottles when making beverages from this section. Seek these out in advance of beginning a project to ensure you are prepared when the brew is ready.

Beverage Fermentation Basics

- **Don't go off course on these recipes just yet.** Before you veer off and create something all your own, be sure that you know the basics. While you may be tempted to lower sugar amounts or change ratios, be advised that this may not yield the desired results. Ferments require sugar to work, and much of this is metabolized during fermentation.

Changing these amounts or using different sugars than called for in these recipes can have negative results, and in some cases, it can ruin your starter culture.

- **Bottling is key.** For most of the recipes in this chapter, it is recommended that you bottle your brew in swing-top bottles for storage. These are ideal because they seal tightly, which helps enable the production of carbon dioxide bubbles in the finished product, giving you the mouthfeel of fizzy effervescence. Just be sure to follow the filling and fermenting directions so you don't end up on the opposite end of the spectrum, with too much bubbly in your finished product.

A NOTE ON KOMBUCHA: *You'll need a SCOBY, or symbiotic culture of bacteria and yeast, to make kombucha. This gelatinous pancake-like culture sits on the sweetened tea to ferment it to perfection. If you know someone who makes kombucha, ask for a spare SCOBY, or purchase one from a supplier listed in the Resources section (page 219) to get started.*

As you make kombucha, your SCOBY will grow, and after a couple of batches you will divide it into two smaller pieces, which will keep fermentation going at the same rate. To store your SCOBY in between batches, place it in a clean quart or pint jar and cover it with plain kombucha. Store in the refrigerator for up to 1 month, bring it back to room temperature, and proceed as usual with the recipe.

KOMBUCHA
TROUBLESHOOTING TIPS

There are many variables that affect kombucha making. In most cases, the concerns that arise are harmless. Check out these troubleshooting tips to determine whether you have actual problems.

There are brown stringy things in my kombucha. This is completely normal. Caused by yeasts, these strings are no problem. But if they become too much for you to bear, you can remove them between batches by rinsing them off your SCOBY, and you can eliminate them from your finished brew by straining it before bottling or serving.

My kombucha tastes like vinegar. You probably let your kombucha ferment for too long, or if it fermented at a higher temperature, the process went more quickly than usual. You can still use your SCOBY to make a new batch, and save the vinegar kombucha to use as a starter, or use it in place of vinegar in your favorite recipes.

My SCOBY sank. This is completely normal and no cause for alarm. Conversely, it is completely normal for a SCOBY to float.

There is a film growing on the top of my kombucha. If the film is gelatinous looking, chances are your kombucha is simply growing another SCOBY. This is particularly common when the SCOBY sinks. Unless there is reason to believe that it is mold, this is completely normal.

My SCOBY has spots. A SCOBY can have a wide variation of colors, sizes, and overall appearances. Spots are not uncommon. The exception to this is when the spots are mold. If you inspect your SCOBY and the spots are not fuzzy or do not otherwise look like mold, chances are good that all is well. If they are mold, discard the kombucha and SCOBY and start again.

There is mold on my SCOBY. Mold is generally pretty easy to spot. It is sometimes green, white, or even brown. Most of the time it is fuzzy looking. If mold grows on your kombucha or SCOBY, discard them both and begin again with fresh ingredients.

starter recipe KOMBUCHA

MAKES 2 QUARTS Prep: **20 minutes** | Fermentation: **7 to 10 days** | Storage: **2 months**

Of all the ferments, kombucha is probably one of the cheapest to make at home. Once you acquire a SCOBY, all that's required is tea and sugar, making the cost of each batch exceedingly low compared to store-bought brands. When you get the process down, you can either drink it plain, or secondary ferment your brews to make delicious concoctions on a par with your favorite store-bought varieties. For your first batch, your kombucha starter will simply come from a bottle of store-bought kombucha. Going forward, you can reserve a cup from your previous batch.

6¾ cups water, divided
½ cup sugar
4 black, green, or white tea bags
1 SCOBY (page 191)
1 cup starter kombucha

1 Bring 2 cups of the water just to boiling in a small saucepan on the stovetop. Add the sugar and stir to dissolve.

2 Add the tea bags to the pan and cover the pan with its lid. Steep for 10 minutes. Use a stainless-steel spoon to squeeze each tea bag against the side of the pot to extract as much tea as possible. Remove the tea bags and discard.

continues ▶

3   Pour the remaining 4¾ cups water into a half-gallon jar or other large nonreactive vessel. Add the tea to the jar, and use a thermometer to ensure that the temperature is 72°F or below. This can also be determined by touch, as the tea should feel cool.

4   Using clean hands, place the SCOBY on the surface of the tea, and add the starter kombucha. Depending on the SCOBY, it may sink or float; this does not make any difference. However, the top of the kombucha or SCOBY should be at least 1 inch below the top of the jar. If there is too much tea in the jar, remove a little with a ladle at this time. Cover the jar with a clean kitchen cloth secured by a rubber band.

5   Store the jar in a location with a constant temperature between 72° and 78°F. Ensure that it is out of the path of direct sunlight.

6   After around 7 days, insert a straw into the kombucha and cap the top with your finger to extract a small amount. Remove the straw from the jar and taste the kombucha. If you like the taste, you are done. If it is still too sweet, continue fermentation until you like the flavor.

Home Fermentation

194

7 With clean hands, remove the SCOBY and place it in a nonreactive bowl if you plan on starting another batch immediately, or in a jar if you don't plan on making more until later. In either case, add 1 cup of the finished kombucha to the bowl or jar to cover the SCOBY.

8 To store the SCOBY for a later batch, place a lid on the jar and refrigerate it for up to 3 weeks. Before using it again, leave the SCOBY on the counter until it comes to room temperature.

9 When the kombucha is done and you are ready to store it, place a funnel over a swing-top bottle and pour or ladle the kombucha into the bottle, leaving about 1 inch headspace. If desired, add additional ingredients to create flavored kombucha (see pages 196 to 199). Cap the bottle and leave it on the counter for a couple more days for secondary fermentation. Refrigerate before serving.

- -

Notes:

- -

A CLOSER LOOK: *Kombucha tends to get some stringy, yeasty pieces in it, which can be unappetizing for many people. If these bother you, use a stainless-steel mesh strainer to strain them away from the liquid before bottling. Alternatively, you can pour the kombucha through a strainer and into a glass when serving.*

MINT KOMBUCHA

Mint is so easy to grow that many people consider it on a par with common weeds. If you happen to have a patch near you, grab a handful and use it to your advantage. Mint is a cooling herb, making this a refreshing blend, especially on a hot afternoon. This simple kombucha uses the same principals of secondary fermentation to create an appealing brew bursting with unexpected flavor.

2 quarts Kombucha (page 193)
16 to 24 mint leaves

1 Prepare 6 bottles for filling. Stuff 2 to 3 mint leaves into each bottle, tearing them as you go.

2 Using a funnel and strainer, pour the kombucha into the bottles, leaving about 2 inches of headspace. Secure the swing-tops and leave to ferment at room temperature for 2 to 3 days. Transfer to the refrigerator to halt fermentation, and serve chilled.

MAKES 2 QUARTS Prep: **15 minutes** | Fermentation: **2 to 3 days** | Storage: **1 month**

Notes:

Help: My SCOBY is Growing!

After you make a batch or two of kombucha, you will find that your SCOBY has multiplied in size, forming a smaller SCOBY on its surface. If you allow the SCOBY to get too big, it will ferment the tea too quickly, making it difficult to keep up with the constantly increasing supply. Therefore, instead of increasing your kombucha consumption considerably, once the SCOBY exceeds an inch or two in size, simply divide it in two—that way you'll have a backup in case your current SCOBY becomes contaminated.

To separate SCOBYs, peel the layers apart into two flat pieces. If they will not come apart easily, they can also be cut with clean kitchen shears. Once they are separated, place one SCOBY in a jar and cover it with kombucha. Add a lid and store it in the refrigerator until you are ready to use it, or share the love and give it away to a friend who wants to start brewing kombucha.

STRAWBERRY-CHIA KOMBUCHA

Popular brands of kombucha have been adding chia seeds to their recipes for years. This extra nutrient boost is strange and gelatinous at first, but once you get over its newness, you'll get hooked on the interesting mouthfeel it creates. Try this simple homemade variation and save big over national brands with just minutes of your time. After you secondary ferment the kombucha with strawberries, you mix in the hydrated chia seeds to complete the drink.

1 quart Kombucha (page 193)
5 strawberries
1 cup cold water
¼ cup chia seeds

1 In a quart jar, combine the kombucha and strawberries, leaving about ½ inch headspace. Cap with a lid tightly and leave at room temperature to ferment for 3 to 5 days. Move the jar to the refrigerator and chill overnight.

2 In a pint jar, combine the water and chia seeds. Stir, cover, and place in the refrigerator for at least 2 hours. The seeds will hydrate and form a gel during this time.

3 Prepare 4 glasses for drinking. Put ¼ cup of the hydrated chia gel in each glass, then strain in 1 cup of kombucha. Stir well and serve.

MAKES 1 QUART

Prep: **5 minutes** | Chilling: **overnight** | Fermentation: **3 to 5 days** | Storage: **1 month**

Notes:

GINGER-PEAR KOMBUCHA

Secondary fermentation is where you can add some serious pizazz to your kombucha. This process creates a fizzy kombucha, especially when completed in an airtight vessel. For the best carbonation and ease of storage, use swing-top bottles, although, in a pinch, a mason jar with a lid can also be used.

1 pear, peeled and cored
1 (2-inch) piece ginger
2 quarts Kombucha (page 193)

1 In a food processor, purée the pear. Cut the piece of ginger in half. Peel one half and slice it into ¼-inch-thick rounds. In a half-gallon jar, combine the kombucha, pear purée, and ginger slices. Apply the lid tightly and leave at room temperature for 24 hours.

2 Prepare 6 swing-top bottles for filling. Peel the remaining piece of ginger and slice it into ¼-inch-thick rounds. Place 1 or 2 slices in each bottle. Using a funnel and strainer, pour the kombucha into the bottles, leaving about 2 inches of headspace. Secure the swing-tops and leave to ferment at room temperature for 1 to 2 more days. Transfer to the refrigerator to halt fermentation, and serve chilled.

Beverages

MAKES 2 QUARTS   Prep: **15 minutes** | Fermentation: **2 to 3 days** | Storage: **1 month**

Notes:

A CLOSER LOOK: *The longer you leave bottled kombucha on the counter for secondary fermentation, especially in ferments with lots of added sugar, the more likely it is for your brew to become alcoholic. For this reason, try not to stretch secondary fermentation beyond 3 days, and do not considerably increase the amount of fruit or fruit juice added. For more sweetness, mix the kombucha with juice or other sweeteners after secondary fermentation.*

WATER KEFIR

If you want to cut back on soda but still want something sweet and delicious to savor throughout the day, water kefir is the way to go. Considered a "natural soda" or soda alternative, this probiotic beverage is dairy free, perfect for people who cannot tolerate dairy kefir. Like kefir and kombucha, water kefir supports gut health and overall wellness. You will need to get some water kefir grains—check out the Resources section (page 219) to get started.

4 cups water, divided

¼ cup sugar

¼ cup rehydrated water kefir grains

1 In a small saucepan, heat 1 cup of the water until it just begins to simmer. Add the sugar and stir to dissolve. Transfer the sugar-water to a quart jar and fill the jar with the remaining 3 cups water. The mixture should be lukewarm. Add the water kefir grains to the jar and cover the jar with a clean kitchen towel secured by a rubber band. Leave the jar at room temperature for 24 to 48 hours.

2 Strain out the grains and begin another batch in the same way. To create fizziness in the brewed batch, transfer it to swing-top bottles or a jar, apply the lid or top, and ferment for an additional day at room temperature. Refrigerate to halt fermentation, and serve chilled.

MAKES 1 QUART Prep: **5 minutes** | Fermentation: **2 to 3 days** | Storage: **1 month**

Notes:

A CLOSER LOOK: *After fermentation, water kefir is mostly flat, with just a touch of effervescence. To transform it into a natural soda-like beverage, proceed to secondary fermentation as described in step 2, at which point you can also add ingredients to boost flavor and create its trademark fizziness. See pages 201 to 203 for some ideas to get you started.*

GINGER SODA WATER KEFIR

With much less sugar than traditional ginger ale, but all the flavor and bite, you really can't go wrong with this naturally fermented stomach soother. Brew up a batch to have on hand during flu season, or simply drink it as part of a regular routine to aid digestion. This tastes great both chilled and at room temperature.

1 quart plain Water Kefir
  (page 200), grains removed
1 (3-inch) piece ginger, peeled and
  cut into ¼-inch-thick rounds

1 In a quart jar, combine the water kefir and ginger. Cap the jar tightly with a lid and leave at room temperature to ferment for 48 hours.

2 Prepare 3 swing-top bottles for filling. Using a funnel and strainer, transfer the water kefir to the bottles. Secure the caps and leave the bottles at room temperature to ferment for an additional 24 hours. Refrigerate to halt fermentation, and serve chilled.

MAKES 1 QUART   Prep: **5 minutes** | Fermentation: **2 to 3 days** | Storage: **1 month**

Notes:

A CLOSER LOOK: *Ginger is a rhizome that stimulates digestion and boosts circulation. It is particularly helpful during cold and flu season when it can help ease congestion in the lungs and assist in relieving aches and pains. When buying fresh ginger, select smaller pieces, as they have more concentrated flavor.*

BLUEBERRY-GINGER WATER KEFIR

Blueberry and ginger is one of my favorite flavor combinations. This pair works together in many ways, be it cooking, baking, jamming, or fermenting. Here, the ginger gives some spiciness to the drink, and blueberries provide a little added sweetness and character. This recipe provides a good amount of ginger for my taste, but feel free to play around with the amount until you find a level that suits your palate.

1 (1-inch) piece ginger

¼ cup blueberries, fresh or frozen, lightly crushed

1 quart plain Water Kefir (page 200), grains removed

1 Cut the piece of ginger in half. Peel one half and slice it into several thin strips. In a quart jar, combine the blueberries, ginger strips, and water kefir. Cover the jar tightly with a lid and leave at room temperature to ferment for 48 hours.

2 Prepare 3 or 4 swing-top bottles. Peel the remaining piece of ginger and slice it into ¼-inch-thick rounds. Place 1 or 2 slices in each bottle. Using a funnel and strainer, pour the water kefir into the bottles and secure the caps. Leave the bottles to ferment at room temperature for another 24 hours. Refrigerate to halt fermentation, and serve chilled.

MAKES 1 QUART   Prep: **10 minutes** | Fermentation: **3 days** | Storage: **1 month**

Notes:

SEASONAL SWAP: *Substitute any of your favorite berries in equal proportions in this recipe. Whether fresh or frozen, any berry that tastes good to you will likely produce good results in water kefir. Experiment with what you have on hand, and try out new flavor combinations for each season.*

BLACKBERRY-SAGE WATER KEFIR

When the weather is cold and gloomy, make use of those blackberries you've got squirreled away in your freezer and whip up a batch of this sunny tonic. If you don't have any frozen blackberries on hand, be sure to stock up next summer. Once you taste this, you'll make certain never to run out again.

¼ cup blackberries, lightly crushed
1 quart plain Water Kefir (page 200), grains removed
8 sage leaves, divided

1 In a quart jar, combine the blackberries, water kefir, and 5 of the sage leaves. Cap the jar tightly with a lid and leave at room temperature to ferment for 48 hours.

2 Prepare 3 swing-top bottles for filling. Using a funnel and strainer, transfer the water kefir to the bottles. Add 1 torn sage leaf to each bottle. Secure the caps and leave the bottles at room temperature to ferment for an additional 24 hours. Refrigerate to halt fermentation, and serve chilled.

MAKES 1 QUART   Prep: **5 minutes** | Fermentation: **2 to 3 days** | Storage: **1 month**

Notes:

Taking a Break from Water Kefir

Like milk kefir grains, water kefir grains can continuously produce back-to-back batches of water kefir. While they don't need a break, sometimes you do. Store water kefir grains in a sugar-water solution (using the same ratio of 4 cups water to ¼ cup sugar) for up to 3 weeks in an airtight container in the refrigerator. When you are ready to begin again, change out the water and proceed as usual. If the resulting water kefir smells and tastes good, it is fine to drink as well.

BLACKBERRY MEAD

This mildly sweet wine, produced from honey and blackberries, makes for a perfect after-dinner treat. Because the production of alcohol requires an anaerobic environment, an airlock is required to create mead. You will need a gallon jug, an airlock, a bung, plastic tubing, and an auto-siphon to complete this project. Check out the Resources section (page 219) to find suppliers who sell these products, or visit your local home brew store, and you will be on your way to making small-scale ferments in the comfort of your own home.

9 cups water

4 cups raw honey

4 cups blackberries

1 package champagne yeast

1 In a large pot, bring the water to just under the boiling point, turn off the heat, and let it cool for a few minutes. Stir in the honey.

2 In a separate bowl, lightly mash the blackberries. Add the fruit to the water-honey mixture, and let it cool until the temperature is below 100°F. This will feel lukewarm to the touch.

3 Using a funnel, transfer the honey-water-berry mixture to the gallon jug. If necessary, rehydrate the yeast before proceeding; follow the package directions to determine if this is needed. Sprinkle the yeast on the surface of the liquid.

4 Fill the airlock with water to the fill line, attach it to the bung, and place it in the jug to create a tight seal. Place the jug in a cool, dark location.

5 After about 2 weeks, test the mead. If you like the flavor at this point, it is done. If you'd like the finished mead to be dry (not sweet), continue to ferment it for up to 2 additional weeks, until you do not notice the taste of sugar. Keep in mind that when bottling mead with a lot of sugar still remaining, this will create carbon dioxide, or carbonation, in the bottle.

6 Prepare 10 to 12 swing-top bottles. Transfer the mead using plastic tubing and an auto-siphon to the bottles, taking care not to disturb the sediment.

7 Cap the bottles and store them until ready for drinking.

MAKES 1 GALLON Prep: **5 minutes** | Fermentation: **2 to 4 weeks** | Storage: **6 to 12 months**

Notes:

RASPBERRY-LEMON SHRUB

With a shrub, virtually any fruit pairing will work well. Here, I created a raspberry-lemon shrub that is bright and flavorful. Like many other fruit ferments, this can be made using frozen berries, so it can brighten your day even in the doldrums of winter. Remember to use organic citrus, especially when including the peel in the ferment, to avoid unnecessary exposure to pesticides and herbicides.

1 cup raspberries

1 organic lemon, halved

1 cup raw apple cider vinegar

¾ cup sugar

1 Put the raspberries in a pint jar. Using a spoon or pestle, lightly tamp down the berries so that they begin to release their juices. Squeeze in the lemon juice from both halves of the lemon, and then place the spent rinds in the jar. Add the vinegar and cover with a clean kitchen towel secured by a rubber band. Leave at room temperature for 24 hours.

2 The next day, add the sugar to the jar. Stir the mixture well. Cover and refrigerate for 7 additional days, shaking the jar occasionally to mix its contents. Serve with a 4-to-1 ratio of water to shrub. Strain out the lemon and berries, if desired, before serving.

MAKES 1½ CUPS   Prep: **5 minutes** | Fermentation: **8 days** | Storage: **2 to 3 months**

Notes:

BLACKBERRY SHRUB

Shrubs are sweet-and-sour fermented treats that make welcomed additions at any occasion. Flavor water with this simple syrupy concoction, add sparkling water to make a soda-like tonic, or add a splash to your favorite cocktail. Whatever you do, just make it! These are so simple and flavorful, you will soon be eyeing all kinds of fruits to use for this addictive drink.

1 cup blackberries
1 cup raw apple cider vinegar
¾ cup sugar
Mint leaves, for garnish

1 Put the blackberries in a pint jar. Using a spoon or pestle, lightly tamp down the berries so that they begin to release their juices. Add the vinegar and cover with a clean kitchen towel secured by a rubber band. Leave at room temperature for 24 hours.

2 The next day, add the sugar to the jar and stir the mixture well. Cover and refrigerate for 7 additional days, shaking the jar occasionally to mix its contents. Serve with a 4-to-1 ratio of water to shrub. If desired, strain out the berries before serving. Garnish with mint leaves and a fresh berry or two.

MAKES 1½ CUPS Prep: **5 minutes** | Fermentation: **8 days** | Storage: **2 to 3 months**

Notes:

RHUBARB SHRUB

One of the first flavors of spring, rhubarb makes a fantastic shrub that, when combined with sugar, is a treat for the taste buds. Sour notes from the rhubarb and vinegar combine to make this a complex sweet-and-sour addition to your treasure trove of drinks. Make this in early spring when rhubarb first becomes available and is most tender.

1 cup diced rhubarb
1 cup raw apple cider vinegar
¾ cup sugar

1 Put the rhubarb in a pint jar. Using a spoon or pestle, lightly tamp down the rhubarb so that it is slightly broken in parts and begins to release a little juice. Add the vinegar and cover with a clean kitchen towel secured by a rubber band. Leave at room temperature for 24 hours.

2 The next day, add the sugar to the jar. Stir the mixture well. Cover and refrigerate for 7 additional days, shaking the jar occasionally to mix its contents. Serve with a 4-to-1 ratio of water to shrub. Strain out the rhubarb before serving.

MAKES 1½ CUPS   Prep: **5 minutes** | Fermentation: **8 days** | Storage: **2 to 3 months**

Notes:

A CLOSER LOOK: *Rhubarb is ready to eat when its red, celery-like stalks appear. A sour and astringent food, it is helpful in removing toxins from the body. It is high in vitamins A and C, as well as potassium. Select stalks that are crisp and plump. Store the stalks in a bag in the crisper drawer of your refrigerator, and use within several days for the best quality.*

CONCORD GRAPE SHRUB

Concord grapes have a wonderfully nostalgic flavor and a distinctly dark color. Their sweetness shines in this simple shrub that is well worth the short wait it takes to make the vibrant creation. Find concord grapes in late summer at farm markets, or find a friend with a vine, as surely they can spare a cluster or two off of this notoriously heavy fruit-bearing variety.

1 cup crushed Concord grapes

¾ cup sugar

1 cup raw apple cider vinegar

1 tablespoon balsamic vinegar

1 In a small bowl, combine the grapes and sugar. Cover the bowl and refrigerate for at least 12 hours or up to 24 hours. Place a strainer over a pint jar and pour the mixture over the strainer, extracting the juice. Use a spoon to mash the grapes further to extract as much juice as possible.

2 Add the vinegars to the jar with the sugary juice, stir well, cover, and refrigerate for 7 days, shaking the jar occasionally. Serve with a 4-to-1 ratio of water to shrub.

MAKES 1½ CUPS Prep: **10 minutes** | Fermentation: **8 days** | Storage: **2 to 3 months**

Notes:

A CLOSER LOOK: *This, like all the other shrubs, pairs well with alcohol for an adult-only drink. My favorite way to serve an alcohol-based shrub drink is with a good whiskey. Mix 1 part whiskey to 2 parts shrub for a delicious drink that works as well on a hot summer day as a cold winter one.*

PLUM-GINGER SHRUB

Plums become ripe about midsummer. Look for the light-colored Shiro plums at farmers' markets or specialty stores, and choose those that are still slightly firm. The ginger really shines along with the plums here in a nearly spicy capacity. Scale the amount up or down depending on your taste. I really like this one bubbly, mixed with sparkling water or Water Kefir (page 200).

1 cup pitted Shiro plum halves
1 (2-inch) piece ginger,
   peeled and sliced
1 cup raw apple cider vinegar
¾ cup sugar
Whole star anise, for garnish

1 Put the plums in a clean pint jar. Using a spoon or pestle, lightly tamp down the plums so they begin to release their juices. Add the ginger slices. Add the vinegar and cover with a clean kitchen towel secured by a rubber band. Leave at room temperature for 24 hours.

2 The next day, add the sugar to the jar and stir the mixture well. Cover and refrigerate for 7 additional days, shaking the jar occasionally to mix its contents. Serve with a 4-to-1 ratio of water to shrub. Strain out the plums and ginger before serving, and garnish each drink with 1 whole star anise.

MAKES 1½ CUPS Prep: **5 minutes** | Fermentation: **8 days** | Storage: **2 to 3 months**

Notes:

A CLOSER LOOK: *Shiro plums are a type of yellow plum that are super juicy and exceptionally sweet. Look for them in markets in late July when they become ripe. If you can't find them, substitute another variety of red or purple plum, which will produce a wonderful red or pink-hued shrub.*

BEET KVASS

In my extremely unscientific study of family and friends, I learned that most people tend to hate beet kvass on first taste. As with many fermented foods, the appreciation of kvass is something that develops over time. I like to make this by the half-gallon, as it stores well and facilitates drinking it on a regular basis. Known for their cleansing abilities, beets are great for managing many chronic conditions and can aid in healthy digestion.

1 pound beets, scrubbed and cut
    into 1-inch chunks
¼ cup whey (page 31) or
    sauerkraut brine (page 41)
2 teaspoons sea salt

1 In a half-gallon jar, combine the beets, whey or sauerkraut brine, and salt. Fill the jar with water, leaving 1 inch of headspace.

2 Cover the jar with a clean kitchen towel secured by a rubber band. Leave the jar at room temperature for 3 to 7 days. When you see bubbles rising in the kvass, it is ready for drinking. Cap the jar and transfer it to the refrigerator to chill. Strain out the beets before serving.

MAKES 2 QUARTS Prep: **10 minutes** | Fermentation: **3 to 7 days** | Storage: **1 month**

Notes:

A CLOSER LOOK: *You can use the same batch of beets for up to two more batches of kvass. To do so, repeat the same steps with the used beets. For added flavor, consider including a few slices of ginger, whole cloves, allspice berries, or cardamom pods to the brew.*

NECTARINE-BLACKBERRY KVASS

In Oregon, stone fruits begin to ripen in August, just around the same time that blackberries hit their peak. Together, these two create a flavorful drink that hits your tongue with carbonation and tempts your senses with the mixture of sweet and slightly sour. Fruit kvass is even easier to produce than most fermented beverages, requiring a minimal amount of kitchen work.

2 large nectarines, halved and pitted

1 cup blackberries

1 tablespoon raw honey

1 (1-inch) piece ginger, peeled and sliced

1 In a quart jar, combine the nectarines, blackberries, honey, and ginger slices. Fill the jar with water, leaving 1 inch of headspace.

2 Cover the jar with a clean kitchen towel secured by a rubber band. Leave the jar at room temperature for 2 to 3 days. When you see bubbles rising vigorously in the kvass, it is ready for drinking. Cap the jar and transfer it to the refrigerator to chill. Strain out the fruit and ginger before serving.

MAKES 1 QUART   Prep: **5 minutes** | Fermentation: **2 to 3 days** | Storage: **1 week**

Notes:

APPENDIX A THE DIRTY DOZEN AND CLEAN FIFTEEN

2015

DIRTY DOZEN	CLEAN FIFTEEN
Apples	Asparagus
Celery	Avocados
Cherry tomatoes	Cabbage
Cucumbers	Cantaloupe
Grapes	Cauliflower
Nectarines	Eggplant
Peaches	Grapefruit
Potatoes	Kiwis
Snap peas	Mangoes
Spinach	Onions
Strawberries	Papayas
Sweet bell peppers	Pineapples
	Sweet corn

In addition to the Dirty Dozen, the EWG added two foods contaminated with highly toxic organo-phosphate insecticides:

Sweet peas (frozen)

Sweet potatoes

Hot peppers

Kale/Collard greens

A nonprofit and environmental watchdog organization called Environmental Working Group (EWG) looks at data supplied by the US Department of Agriculture (USDA) and the Food and Drug Administration (FDA) about pesticide residues and compiles a list each year of the best and worst pesticide loads found in commercial crops. You can refer to the Dirty Dozen list to know which fruits and vegetables you should always buy organic. The Clean Fifteen list lets you know which produce is considered safe enough when grown conventionally to allow you to skip the organics. This does not mean that the Clean Fifteen produce is pesticide-free, though, so wash these fruits and vegetables thoroughly. These lists change every year, so make sure you look up the most recent before you fill your shopping cart. You'll find the most recent lists as well as a guide to pesticides in produce at EWG.org/FoodNews.

MEASUREMENT CONVERSIONS

VOLUME EQUIVALENTS (LIQUID)

US STANDARD	US STANDARD (OUNCES)	METRIC (APPROXIMATE)
2 tablespoons	1 fl. oz.	30 mL
¼ cup	2 fl. oz.	60 mL
½ cup	4 fl. oz.	120 mL
1 cup	8 fl. oz.	240 mL
1½ cups	12 fl. oz.	355 mL
2 cups or 1 pint	16 fl. oz.	475 mL
4 cups or 1 quart	32 fl. oz.	1 L
1 gallon	128 fl. oz.	4 L

OVEN TEMPERATURES

FAHRENHEIT (F)	CELSIUS (C) (APPROXIMATE)
250	120
300	150
325	165
350	180
375	190
400	200
425	220
450	230

VOLUME EQUIVALENTS (DRY)

US STANDARD	METRIC (APPROXIMATE)
⅛ teaspoon	.5 mL
¼ teaspoon	1 mL
½ teaspoon	2 mL
¾ teaspoon	4 mL
1 teaspoon	5 mL
1 tablespoon	15 mL
¼ cup	59 mL
⅓ cup	79 mL
½ cup	118 mL
⅔ cup	156 mL
¾ cup	177 mL
1 cup	235 mL
2 cups or 1 pint	475 mL
3 cups	700 mL
4 cups or 1 quart	1 L
½ gallon	2 L
1 gallon	4 L

WEIGHT EQUIVALENTS

US STANDARD	METRIC (APPROXIMATE)
½ ounce	15 g
1 ounce	30 g
2 ounces	60 g
4 ounces	115 g
8 ounces	225 g
12 ounces	340 g
16 ounces or 1 pound	455 g

GLOSSARY

Acetobacter aceti: The type of bacteria responsible for transforming alcohol into acetic acid, commonly known as vinegar.

Aerobic: Requiring oxygen for metabolism. In fermentation, this is a term used to describe bacteria and yeast that depend on oxygen for survival.

Airlock: A small piece of equipment used in fermentation that allows for the escape of carbon dioxide, while preventing the entrance of oxygen. In home fermentation, these are typically filled with water to allow for this one-way pathway.

Anaerobic: Requiring the absence of oxygen for metabolism. In fermentation, this term refers to bacteria and yeast that thrive only in the absence of oxygen.

Brine: A solution made most often with salt and water, used in the preservation of food to prevent the growth of harmful bacteria and encourage the growth of beneficial bacteria.

Dry-salting: Rubbing a food item with salt, as opposed to submerging it in a brine.

Fermentation vessel: Any container used for the purpose of fermenting foods or beverages. Must be nonreactive and food-safe.

Headspace: The air space left at the top of a jar or bottle when filling.

Kefir: A fermented cow's milk product that has a similar taste to yogurt but with a thinner consistency, making it suitable for drinking.

Kombucha: A drink made through the fermentation of sweet tea using a SCOBY.

Lactobacillus: The predominant bacteria responsible for lacto-fermentation.

Lacto-fermentation: The conversion of glucose into lactic acid molecules.

Mother culture: A substance that harbors desirable microbes used to inoculate foods or beverages with these same desirable microbes.

Nonreactive: Any substance that does not react in an acidic environment. In cooking, this refers to stainless steel, glass, wood, and some enameled containers or utensils.

Pasteurization: A low-temperature heat-treatment method used in the production of milk to eliminate dangerous pathogens.

Raw food: Any foods that are not heated above 120°F, the temperature at which native enzymes become inactivated. This includes fermented, sprouted, and dehydrated foods when these foods have not been cooked.

SCOBY: A symbiotic culture of bacteria and yeast, used to make kombucha; this culture is a gelatinous, pancake-like patty.

Starter culture: A preparation of living bacteria and yeasts used to inoculate milk, vegetables, and fruits for fermentation. Commonly used in the production of cheese.

Whey: A watery liquid drained from curds during cheese production. When whey is used for the fermentation of other foods, it must be drained from milk products that have not been heated past 120°F, such as kefir and yogurt.

Wild fermentation: The fermentation of foods or beverages using wild yeasts and bacteria, as opposed to inoculating the food items with a starter culture.

Yeast: Microorganisms used to create alcohol in wine and beer making, carbon dioxide in baking, and other changes in a wide variety of food items.

RESOURCES

Wine- and Beer-Making Books

Christensen, Emma. *True Brews: How to Craft Fermented Cider, Beer, Wine, Sake, Soda, Mead, Kefir, and Kombucha at Home.* Berkeley, CA: Ten Speed Press, 2013.

Cox, Jeff. *From Vines to Wines: The Complete Guide to Growing Grapes and Making Your Own Wine.* North Adams, MA: Storey Publishing, 2015.

Hughes, Steve. *The Homebuilt Winery: 43 Projects for Building and Using Winemaking Equipment.* North Adams, MA: Storey Publishing, 2012.

Palmer, John J. *How to Brew: Everything You Need to Know to Brew Beer Right the First Time.* Boulder, CO: Brewers Publications, 2006.

Papazian, Charlie. *The Complete Joy of Homebrewing.* New York: William Morrow, 2014.

Warrick, Sheridan. *The Way to Make Wine: How to Craft Superb Table Wines at Home.* Oakland: University of California Press, 2010.

Fermenting Supplies

Caldwell Bio Fermentation
www.caldwellbiofermentation.com/en/starter-culture.html

Cultures for Health
www.culturesforhealth.com

Pickl-It
www.pickl-it.com

Brewing Supplies

E. C. Kraus
www.eckraus.com

F. H. Steinbart
www.fhsteinbart.com

REFERENCES

Childs, Eric and Jessica. *Kombucha!: The Amazing Probiotic Tea That Cleanses, Heals, Energizes, and Detoxifies.* New York: Avery, 2013.

Fallon, Sally. *Nourishing Traditions: The Cookbook That Challenges Politically Correct Nutrition and the Diet Dictocrats.* White Plains, MD: Newtrends Publishing, 2003.

Foroutan, Robin. "The History and Health Benefits of Fermented Foods." *Food & Nutrition.* Accessed July 28, 2015. www .foodandnutrition.org/Winter-2012/ The-History-and-Health-Benefits-of- Fermented-Food/.

Gardeners and Farmers of Terre Vivante. *Keeping Food Fresh: Old-World Techniques and Recipes.* White River Junction, VT: Chelsea Green, 1999.

Hilimire, Matthew R. "Fermented Foods, Neuroticism, and Social Anxiety: An Interaction Model." *Psychiatry Research* 228, no. 2 (2015), 203–8. doi:10.1016/j .psychres.2015.04.023.

Karlin, Mary. *Mastering Fermentation: Recipes for Making and Cooking with Fermented Foods.* Berkeley, CA: Ten Speed Press, 2013.

Lee, Stephen. *Kombucha Revolution: 75 Recipes for Homemade Brews, Fixers, Elixirs, and Mixers.* Berkeley, CA: Ten Speed Press, 2014.

Lewin, Alex. *Real Food Fermentation: Preserving Whole Fresh Food with Live Cultures in Your Home Kitchen.* Beverly, MA: Quarry Books, 2012.

Midwife Thinking. "The Human Microbiome: Considerations for Pregnancy, Birth, and Early Mothering." Accessed July 28, 2015. www.midwifethinking.com/2014/01/15/ the-human-microbiome-considerations-for- pregnancy-birth-and-early-mothering/.

Selhub, Eva M., Alan C. Logan, and Alison C. Bested. "Fermented Foods, Microbiota, and Mental Health: Ancient Practice Meets Nutritional Psychiatry." *Journal of Physiological Anthropology* 33 no. 1 (2014): 2. Accessed July 28, 2015. doi:10.1186/1880-6805-33-2.

Wood, Rebecca. *The New Whole Foods Encyclopedia.* New York: Penguin, 2010.

Zeidrich, Linda. *The Joy of Pickling: 250 Flavor-Packed Recipes for Vegetables and More from Garden or Market.* Boston: Harvard Common Press, 2009.

RECIPE INDEX

INDEX

Index

Index

About the Author

Katherine Green is a writer and food educator based in Portland, OR. She is a fermentation geek, trained winemaker, and the former owner of Mama Green's Jam. This is her fifth book. She lives with her husband, two sons, and a flock of chicken.

CPSIA information can be obtained
at www.ICGtesting.com
Printed in the USA
BVOW10s0953120816

458846BV00023B/99/P